I0831115

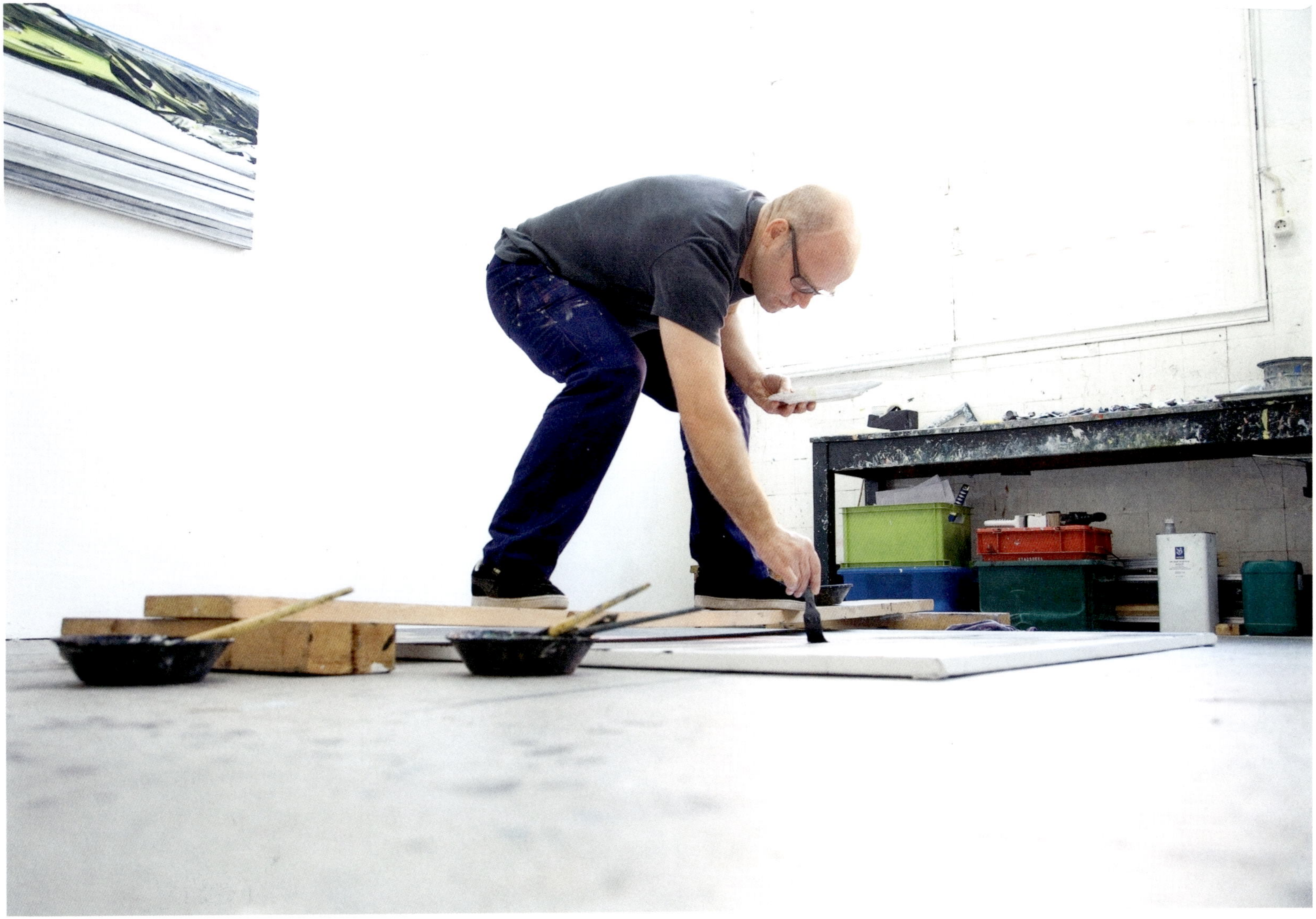

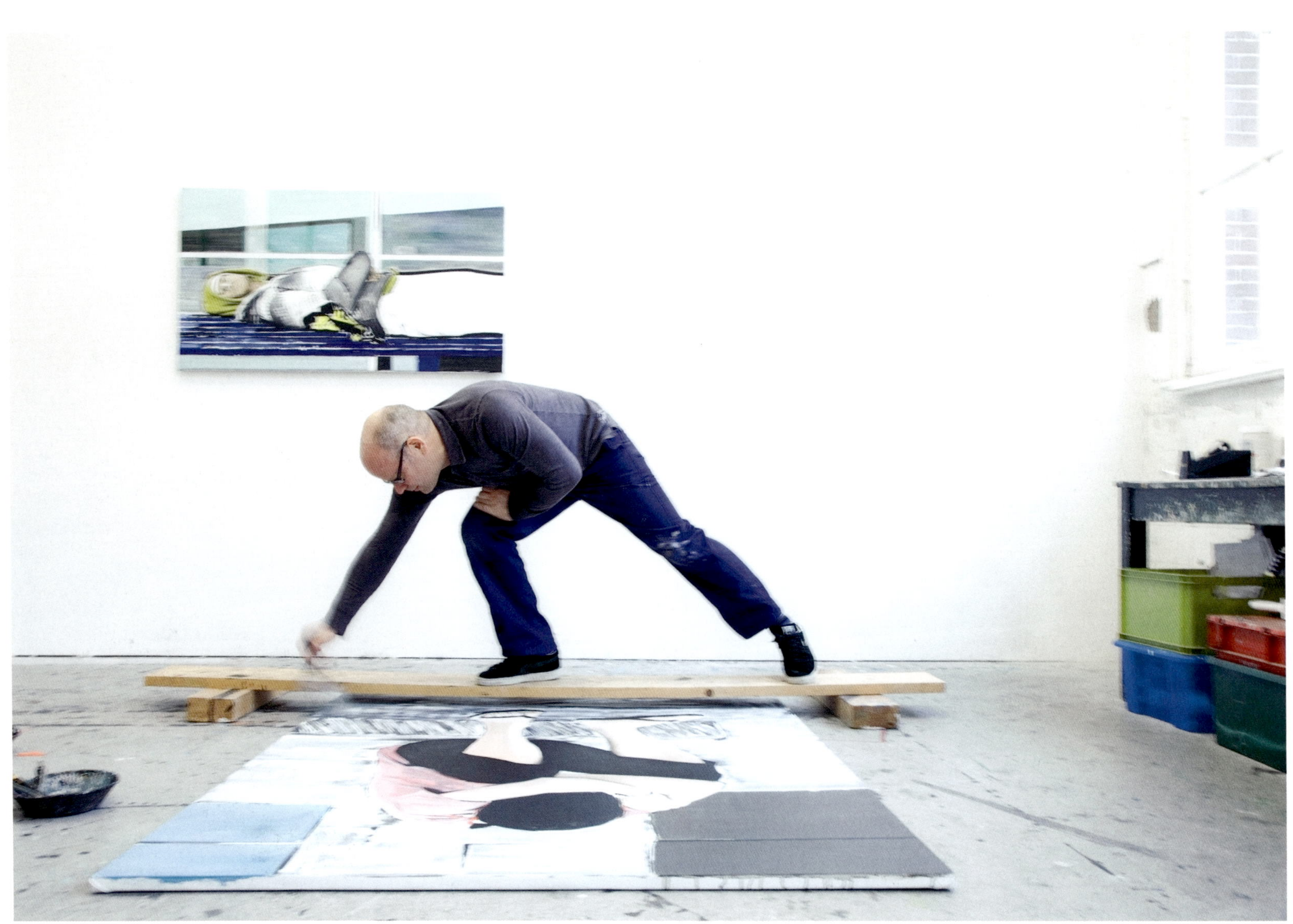

KOEN VERMEULE

Dreamer

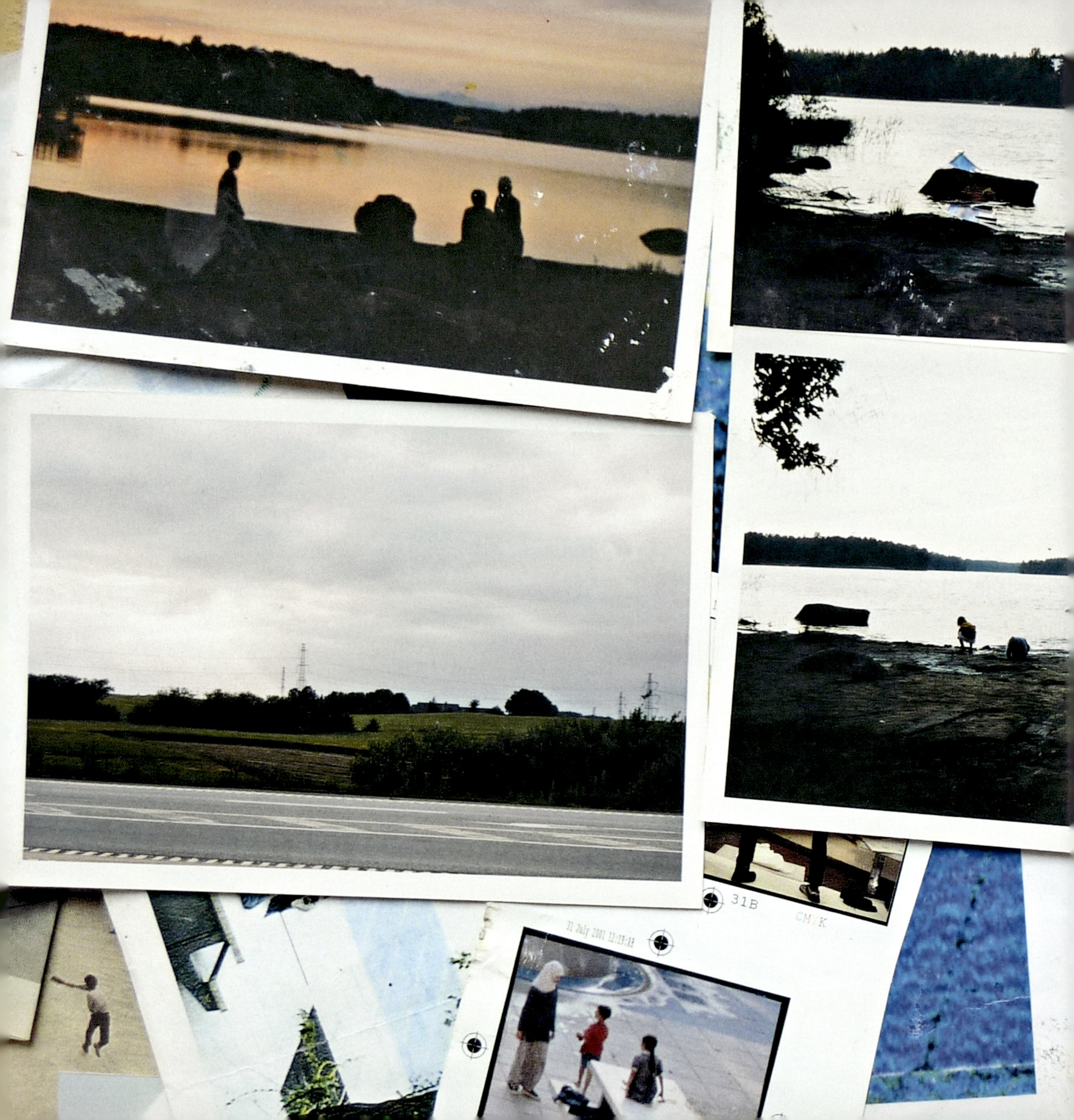
31B
CMYK
31 July 2001

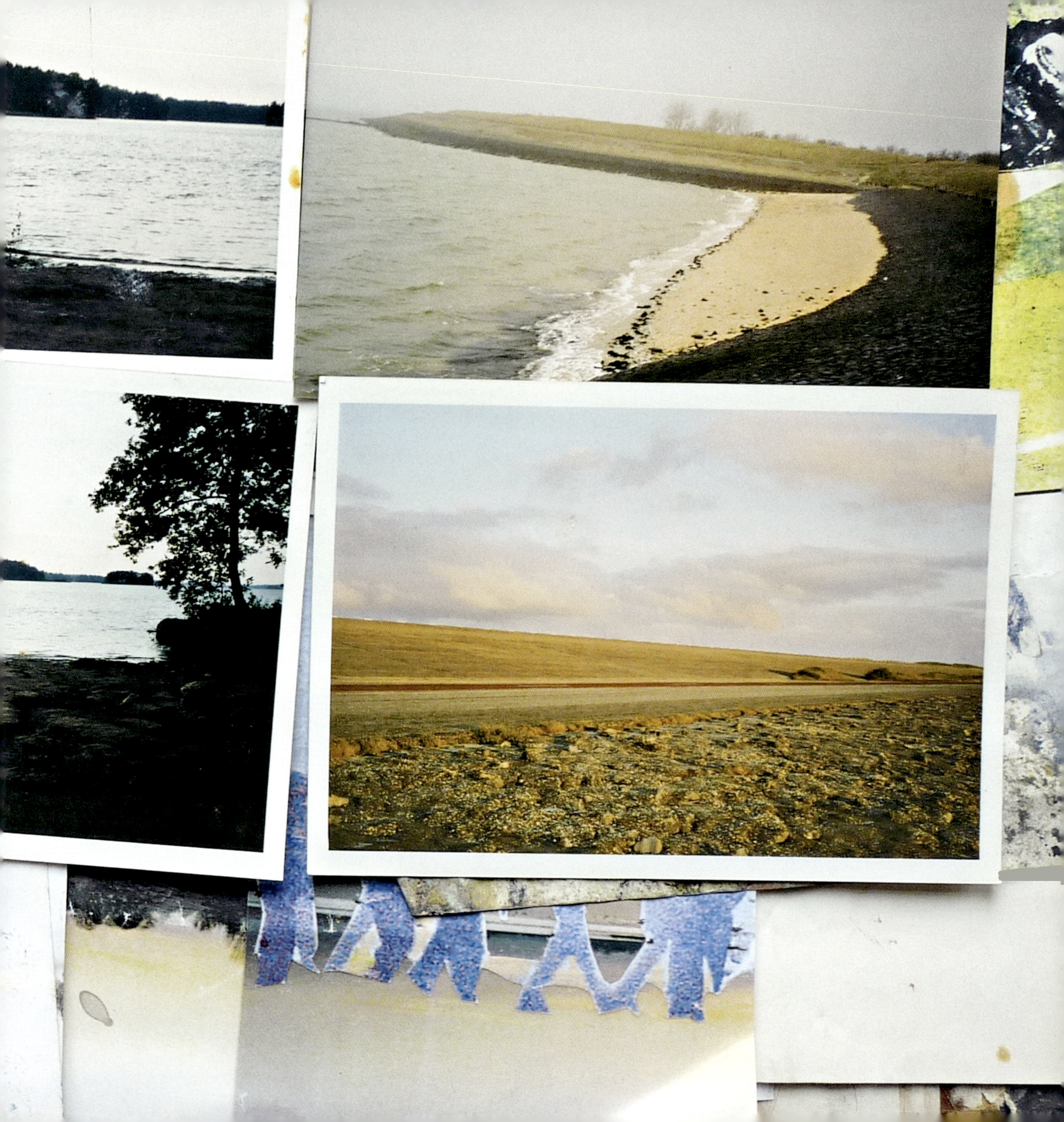

Gedankenaustausch | Exchange of Thoughts

Koen Vermeule & Eckhard Hollmann

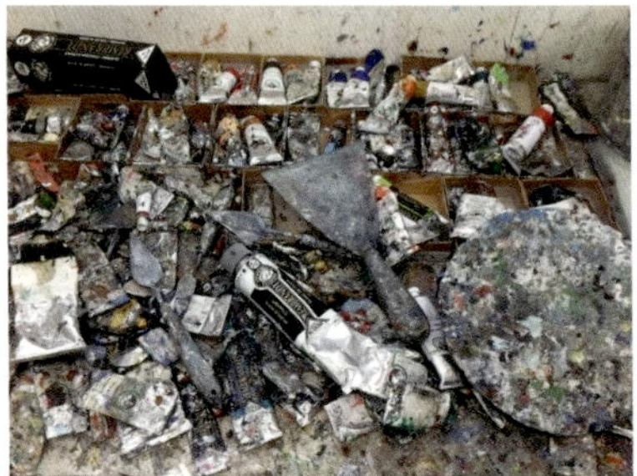

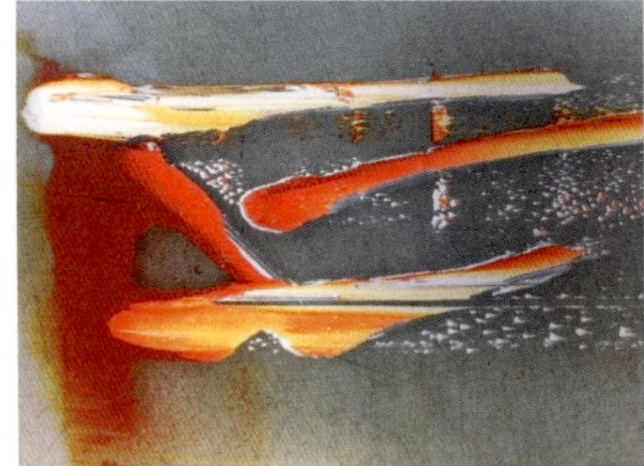

Eine Deiner Ausstellungen hieß „Out and about". Du nanntest das in einem Interview „einen guten Titel für mein gesamtes Werk". Du bist ständig unterwegs, weltweit von Tokio bis Berlin. Liegen die Anfänge Deiner Bilder sozusagen auf der Straße?

Der Titel „Out and about" klingt prosaisch, das liebe ich. Könnte auch ein Magazin sein, das Städte vorstellt, etwa nach dem Motto: „Was gibt es diese Woche in London?" Ich liebe es, durch die Stadt zu gehen oder auf Reisen zu sein, Eindrücke zu sammeln und dann zurück ins Atelier, an die Arbeit! Das macht mich zufrieden.

Du nimmst ja ganz unterschiedliche Motive aus Deiner Umgebung auf. Was interessiert Dich darin am meisten, gibt es eine „Rangordnung"?

Nein, alles muss möglich sein, aber ich habe das nie analysiert. Ich reagiere eher spontan, unbewusst. Meist sind es Plätze, die zunächst mal gar nicht so viele Informationen hergeben, es muss jedenfalls etwas mit mir passieren, etwas muss mich anstoßen. Ich weiß nicht genau, was ich mit meinen Bildern sage, aber ich will etwas sagen über das Jetzt., über unsere Zeit. Nehmen wir ein Beispiel: Massen von Leuten reden auf dem Flugplatz in ihre Handys, aber jeder ist ganz für sich. Oder es gibt wunderschöne Spiegelungen auf dem Boden, der dadurch fast wie eine große Wasserfläche wirkt. Das nutze ich sogar in meiner Landschaftsmalerei.

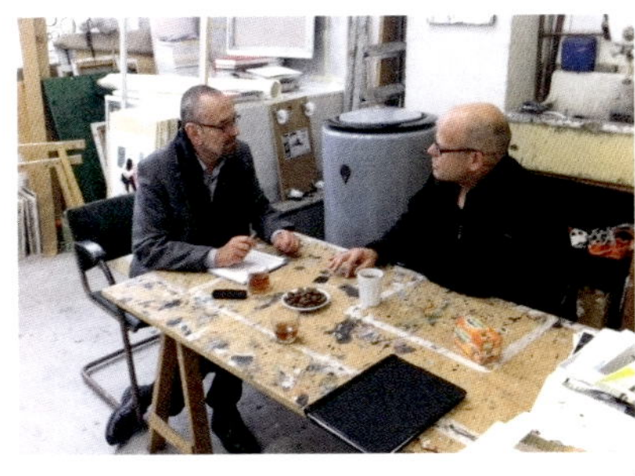

Großstädtische Themen und Straßenszenen beschäftigen Dich offenbar sehr. Gibt es auch eine Verbindung zu Street Art?

Das ist Teil des städtischen Lebens, na klar! Ich habe sogar fast ein Jahr mein Atelier mit einem jungen Sprayer oder besser „Street-Artist" geteilt und sogar versucht, mit ihm gemeinsam Bilder zu malen. Das hat aber nicht funktioniert, die künstlerischen Elemente blieben einander zu fremd. Ein Sammler hat gesagt: „ Wenn zwei in der Kunst zusammengehen, muss eins und eins drei ergeben." Bei uns ist es aber bei der Zwei geblieben.

One of your exhibitions was called "Out and about". In an interview you said it was "a good title for my entire work." You are always on the move, traveling across the world from Tokyo to Berlin. Do your pictures begin, so to speak, on the road?

The title "Out and about" sounds very mundane, and I like that. It could also be a magazine that presents cities, something like: "What's on this week in London?" I love walking through the city and traveling, gathering impressions and then returning to my studio and getting down to work. It makes me happy.

You select very different subjects from your surroundings. What interests you most? Do you have an "order of preference"?

No, everything has to be possible, but I've never analyzed it. I tend to react spontaneously, almost unconsciously. Mostly they are places which at first sight don't seem to provide so much information, but anyway something has to happen to me, something needs to prompt me. I don't know exactly what I'm saying with my pictures, but I want to say something about the here and now, about the times we live in.

Let's take just one example. Masses of people at the airport are talking into their mobile phones, but they are all in their own little worlds. Or there are beautiful reflections on the floor which make it look almost like a vast expanse of water. I even use that in my landscape paintings.

The subject of big cities and street scenes clearly interests you greatly. Are there any links there to street art?

It's a part of city life, of course! I actually shared my studio for almost a year with a young sprayer, or rather a "street artist," and even attempted to paint some pictures with him. But it didn't work; the artistic elements remained too foreign to each other. A collector once said: "When two artists decide to work together, one and one need to make three." But for us the result was always two.

Menschen - oft im Profil gezeigt - spielen in Deinen Bildern eine große Rolle?

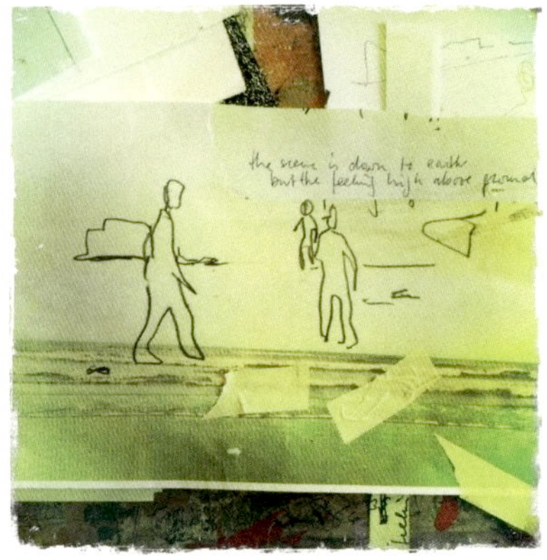

Ein städtischer Platz ist wie eine Kulisse im Theater, darin sitzen, stehen, liegen die Menschen, das Ganze wirkt auf mich kontemplativ, strahlt manchmal sogar etwas von Todesnähe aus.
Einmal wollte ich eine Ausstellung im Musée d' Orsay sehen, davor standen Massen von Leuten. Am Rande sieht man oft Figuren, die ganz in sich versunken sind, gar nicht mehr zu der großen Gruppe gehören. Das gibt viel Freiraum für Interpretation. Meine Bilder sollen dem Betrachter diesen Raum geben. Das Subjekt ist eigentlich außerhalb des Bildes. Denn wir können träumen über Dinge, die wir nicht wissen.

People - often shown in profile - play an important part in your pictures?

A city square is like a stage setting. In it the people sit or stand, or even lie. For me the whole scene has a contemplative feel; it sometimes even radiates a feeling of the proximity of death.
Once I wanted to go to see an exhibition at the Musée d' Orsay and there were crowds of people outside. On the fringes you often see people who are entirely caught up in their own thoughts and who no longer belong to the main group. That provides plenty of space for interpretation. My pictures aim to give the viewer this space. The subject is actually outside the picture. Because we can dream about things that we don't know.

Das Aufteilen, Aufrastern von Bildräumen ist sehr wichtig für Deine Kunst, oder?

Ja, sowohl im Porträt als auch in der Landschaft und in den Straßenszenen. Das findet sich ja in allen Epochen der Kunstgeschichte, auch in der klassischen Moderne und der abstrakten Kunst. Auch dort gibt es viele Dinge, die ich liebe, zum Beispiel die Bilder von Piet Mondrian. Eigentlich versuche ich in meiner Arbeit, diverse Elemente zusammenzubringen. Dabei habe ich aber nie das Gefühl, irgendwelche Versatzstücke zu benutzen. Ich konnte meinen Weg finden, auch wenn es, von heute aus betrachtet, harte Brüche gab. Die Generation vor mir dachte und arbeitete viel formeller als meine Generation. Speziell mit einigen Künstlern in Holland, Deutschland und Polen fühle ich mich sehr verbunden. Das hat mit der Art und Weise zu tun, wie die im Leben stehen, nach bestimmten Dingen gucken und sie für ihre Kunst gebrauchen. Neulich habe ich in München ein großes Gemälde von Florian Thomas gesehen, das einen Campingplatz zeigt. Ich denke, dass

You find it important to divide up the spaces within your pictures, to create a raster?

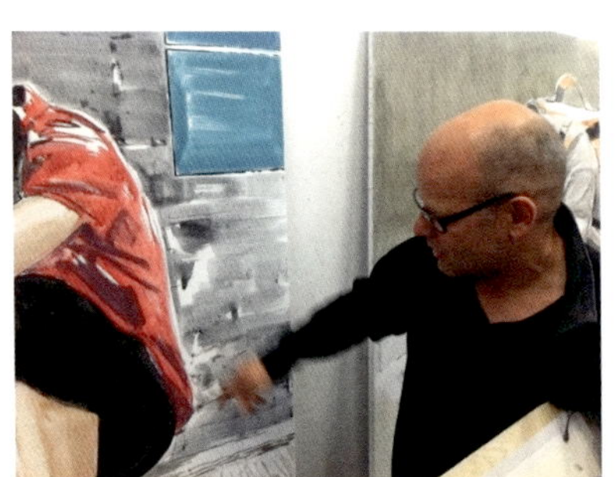

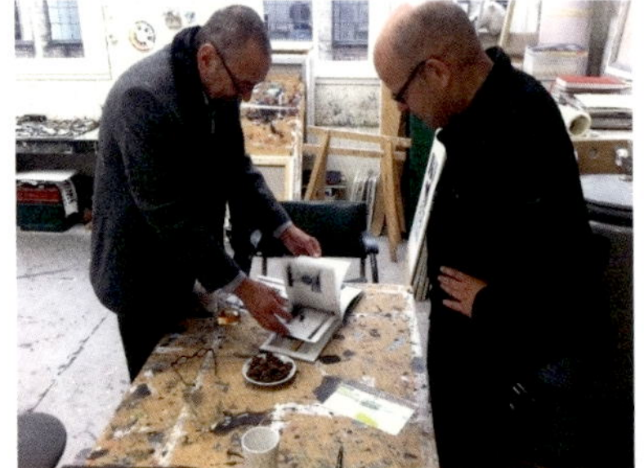

Yes, I do it in portraits as well as in landscapes and street scenes. You can find it in all epochs throughout art history, including Classical Modernism and abstract art. There are things there that I love, like for example the pictures of Piet Mondrian. In my work I actually try to combine various different elements. But I never have the feeling that I'm using clichés. I have managed to find my own way, even if, seen from today's perspective, there were a number of major hiatuses. The generation before me thought and worked much more formally than my generation. I feel I have very close links with certain artists in Holland, Germany, and Poland. It has to do with the way they approach life, how they look at certain things and use art for their own purposes. Recently I saw a big picture by Florian Thomas in Munich that showed a campsite. I think it demonstrates tremendous freedom to be able to produce a big picture of a campsite! Twenty years ago it would have been impossible.

es eine große Freiheit bedeutet, wenn es möglich ist, ein großes Gemälde von einem Campingplatz zu machen! Das wäre vor 20 Jahren noch unmöglich gewesen.

Zeichnest Du vor, mit weichem Stift direkt auf die Leinwand oder mit dünnen Linien in Acrylfarben? Wie funktioniert bei Dir der Prozess der Bildfindung?

Manchmal beginne ich einfach zu malen. *(weist auf eine begonnen Arbeit)* Hier habe ich das zum Beispiel getan. Aber die Figur geriet mir zu groß, ich habe alles noch mal von vorn gemacht. Mein eigentliches Medium der Vorbereitung ist die Fotografie. Monate später im Studio fange ich erst mit der Umsetzung an. Oft gibt es viel mehr auf dem Foto als dann auf das Bild kommt. In so einer Hose *(weist auf das Bild „Dreamer")* gibt es viel mehr Licht und Plastizität, mir passt aber eine flache Form ins Bild. Dann male ich die Hose eben ganz anders.

Es müssen natürlich nicht unbedingt Fotos als Vorlagen da sein. Ich habe auch immer gezeichnet, bereits als Kind in der Schule. Später wäre ich gern selber Zeichenlehrer geworden. Ich habe in einem Innenarchitektenbüro gezeichnet und abends meine Bilder gemalt. Aber das ging nicht, das war zuviel und zu schwer. Dann habe ich mich doch für die *Rijksakademie* beworben und bin angenommen worden. Das war phantastisch, hervorragend.

„The call" von 2008 scheint mir ein sehr „malerisches" Bild zu sein, das ganz auf die Valeurs, auf den Duktus der Farbe setzt. Andere Bilder, wie „West 1" von 2001 erscheinen überaus grafisch, die Farbe ist hier eher im Sinne von Kolorit genutzt. Wie ist das Verhältnis von Farbe und Zeichnung in Deinen Bildern?

Ich beginne immer mit einer Arbeit auf Papier. Dann bin ich freier, da passieren immer Dinge, die mich überraschen. Das ist wie spielen. Farbe läuft runter, es entsteht plötzlich ein Licht an den Kanten und anderes. Es ist nicht so einfach, diese Freiheit dann im großem Format zu bewahren. Ich will das, was auf dem Papier passiert, auch im Gemälde haben, ich bemühe mich, dass die Struk-

Do you sketch out your picture first with a soft pencil directly onto the canvas, or do you draw thin lines in acrylic paint? How do you go about creating a picture?

Sometimes I just start to paint. *(Points to a work in progress.)* That is what I did here, for example. But the figure came out larger than I intended so I simply started again.

The medium which I use to prepare my pictures is really photography. I actually start working on it months later in my studio. Often there is much more on the photo than I end up using in the picture. Trousers like that *(pointing to the picture "Dreamer")* actually have much more light and three-dimensionality, but a flat shape fitted in with my picture better. So I just paint the trousers differently.

Of course, I don't have to have photos as a model to follow. I have always drawn, even as a child during my schooldays. Later I wanted to be a drawing teacher. I drew in an interior designer's office and then painted my own pictures during the evenings. But it didn't work; it was too much and too difficult. Then I applied to the *Rijksakademie* and was accepted. It was fantastic, great.

"The call" of 2008 seems to me to be a very "painterly" picture, one that focuses entirely on the values, the characteristic style of the paint. Other pictures, like "West 1" of 2001, appear more graphical, and in them color is used more in the sense of mood. What is the relationship between color and drawing in your pictures?

I start with a work on paper. There I am free and things that surprise me always happen. It's like playing a game. The paint runs down, and suddenly there is a light on the edges, and things like that. It isn't so easy to maintain this freedom in the large format. I want the things which occur on paper also to happen in the painting. I try to make sure the structures remain open so that a shimmering light is created.

You also work with shapes which you have cut out and which you place on the picture background of your picture?

Yes, it's a process. I cover up certain things and then I go over them with my paintbrush so that you get these painterly effects at the edges. You could describe the result as "frozen moments." The forms flow and yet are

turen offen bleiben, dass ein flirrendes Licht entsteht.

Du arbeitest auch mit ausgeschnittenen Formen, die Du auf dem Bildgrund platzierst?

Ja, das ist ein Prozess. Ich decke bestimmte Dinge ab, dann gehe ich mit dem Pinsel darüber, sodass es an den Kanten zu malerischen Effekten kommt. Was so entsteht, könnte man „gefrorene Momente" nennen. Die Formen fließen, sind aber auch statisch. Aus diesem Kontrast leben die Bilder. Manchmal überklebe ich die Figuren auch vollständig und arbeite am Hintergrund. Dann verdichtet sich das Bild von Schritt zu Schritt immer stärker. Schwarz wird zum Beispiel immer schöner, wenn man mehrere Schichten übereinander legt.

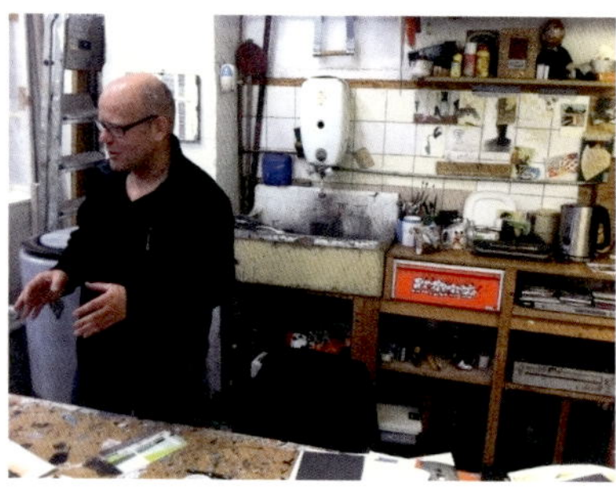

Weißt Du immer, wann Du aufhören musst?

Es ist wirklich Intuition. Der Punkt ist erreicht, wenn es einfach nicht mehr möglich ist, etwas hinzuzufügen.

Kann es auch passieren, dass Du ein Bild verwirfst?

Ja, das kann manchmal sogar sehr schnell gehen und dann beginne ich ganz von vorn. Manchmal probiere ich aber auch weiter mit dem Vorhandenen, in der Hoffnung, dass etwas Neues entsteht.

Sind Mensch und Landschaft für Dich gleichwertige Motive?

Ich war mal mit einem Freund in einem Naturschutzgebiet in Holland unterwegs. *(holt das Bild „Sunset Blue")* Er fragte mich, ob es möglich sei, nach dieser Reise ein adäquates Bild zu machen. War sehr schwer! Dieses Boot führt den Betrachter in die Landschaft. Man kann es aber auch als abstraktes Element lesen.

Der Gegensatz zwischen grafischer und malerischer Haltung ist hier extrem. Ich finde es mutig, in eine „realistische" Landschaft eine so stark abstrahierte Form einzusetzen.

Ich denke, das baut einen schönen Spannungsbogen auf. Der Kontrast zur abstrahierten Form gibt dem Wasser so etwas wie magische Kraft.

Also ein Bild ganz im romantischen Sinne?

Ja, genau.

Deine Landschaften sind sehr streng gegliedert. Die Horizontalen und die Diagonalen wirken am stärksten.

Ja, das hat aber immer realistische Vorbilder. Da ist zum Beispiel ein Deich, den man mit

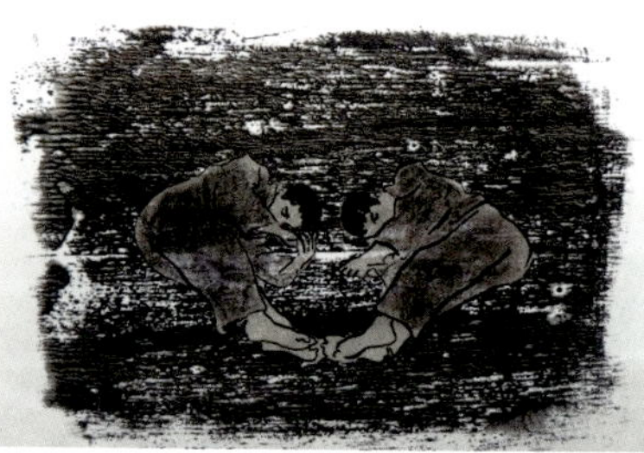

static. This is the contrast from which my pictures live.

Sometimes I glue something over the figures completely and work on the background. Then the picture becomes progressively denser, and denser. Black, for example, becomes more and more beautiful if you paint several layers on wof each other.

Do you always know when you should stop?

It's really intuition. You reach the point when it simply isn't possible to add anything else.

Does it ever happen that you reject a picture entirely?

Yes; sometimes it happens very quickly, and then I start from the beginning again. But sometimes I keep on trying with what I have already produced, in the hope that something new will arise.

Are people and landscapes equally important subjects?

Once I was visiting a nature conservation area in Holland with a friend. *(Fetches the picture Sunset Blue.)* He asked me if it would be possible to paint a picture after the journey which would do justice to what he had seen. It was very difficult! This boat carries the viewer into the landscape. But you can also read it as an abstract element.

The contrast between graphical and painterly attitude is extreme here. I find it very brave to set such a strongly abstracted form into a "realistic" landscape.

I think it creates a nice arc of suspense. The contrast with the abstracted form gives the water something resembling a magical power.

So it's a picture in the Romantic sense?

Yes, exactly.

Your landscapes are very rigidly divided into sections. The horizontal and diagonal lines seem to be the strongest.

Yes; it always has realistic models. There is, for example, a pond which you can drive through in a car, and which at the same time creates an almost abstract form. Really I want to make my paintings clear and powerful; the content must not be closed in and conclusive.

In the 1980s it was claimed that painting was dead; in the last decade it has experienced a surprising renaissance.

Perhaps the road had become too narrow. Artists returned to the everyday objects, to the trivial. I believe that is the new intimacy.

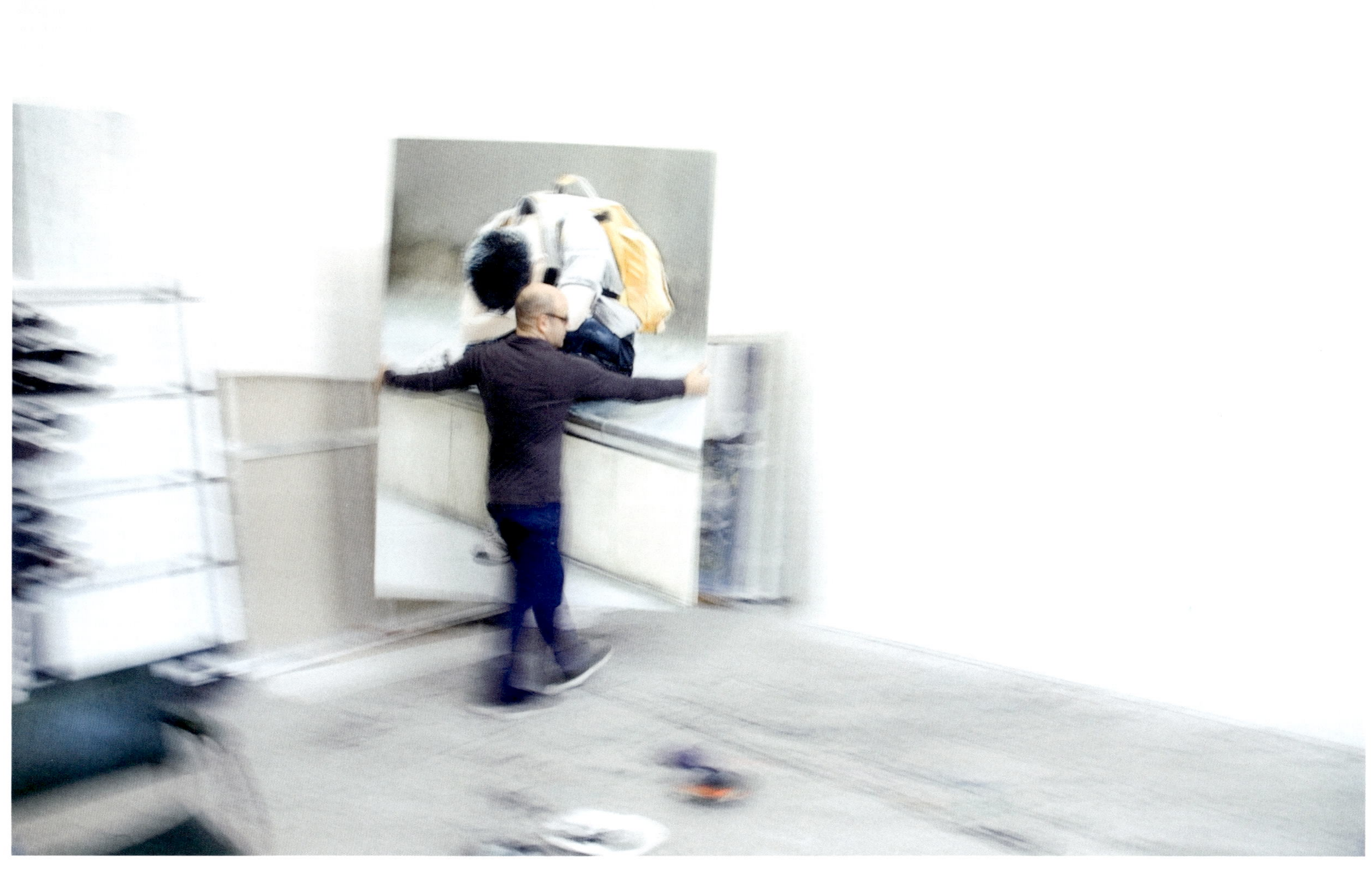

einem Wagen befahren kann, zugleich bildet er eine fast abstrakte Form. Eigentlich will ich meine Gemälde klar und kräftig machen, der Inhalt muss nicht geschlossen und eindeutig sein.

Die Malerei wurde in den 80er Jahren totgesagt, in den letzten zehn Jahren hat sie eine überraschende Renaissance erlebt. Was sind die Ursachen dieser Entwicklung?

Vielleicht war die Straße zu eng geworden. Die Künstler kehrten wieder zurück zum Alltäglichen, auch zum Banalen. Ich glaube, das ist eine neue Intimität. Das Zeitalter der großen pathetischen Themen ist vorbei. Man konzentriert sich auf das eigene Leben, die Freunde, Familie usw.

Aber das begründet doch nicht die neuen Ehren, die Malerei heute erfährt. Warum reichen die modernen Mittel Foto, Video usw. nicht aus?

Videoarbeiten haben mir gezeigt, dass bestimmte Konstellationen, die ich nicht auf die Straße finden kann, im Studio doch zu organisieren und arrangieren sind. So entstehen neue Möglichkeiten für meine Malerei. Ich mag Videos sehr, muss aber unbedingt sagen, dass Malerei viele Male intimer ist. Man kann fühlen, dass das gemalte Bild durch die Sinne gegangen ist und nicht durch eine Maschine. Ich war in Italien, wollte unbedingt die *Heimsuchung* von Jacopo da Pontormo in Florenz sehen. Vorher besuchte ich die Biennale in Venedig. Dort gab es ein großes Video zum selben Thema von Bill Viola. Es hat mir gut gefallen, aber wenn ich es zehnmal gesehen habe, ist es für mich erledigt. Aber das Bild von Pontormo könnte ich mir sicher auch in 100 Jahren noch mit großem Gewinn anschauen.

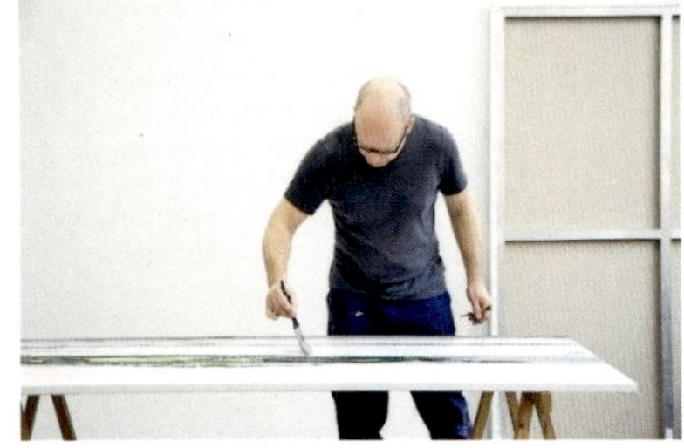

Der Film: „De zachte Weg" zeigt sechs Judokämpfer auf einem Planquadrat. Dazu gibt es Bilder von Dir, die Filmstills sein könnten. Stammt der Film auch von Dir?

Ja, ich hatte ein Drehbuch, das habe ich abgearbeitet. Es ging mir darum, wie die Figuren zueinander stehen, wie sie sich bewegen. Nach dem Film habe ich die Bilder gemalt, das Licht ist ein Spätmittagslicht mit starken Schlagschatten. Ich glaube, das war eine wichtige Arbeit für mich.

What are the causes of this development?

The age of the great pathetic themes is over. People are concentrating on their own lives, their friends and families and so on.

But that still doesn't explain the new accolades which painting is being awarded today. Why are the modern media like photos, video etc. not sufficient here?

Video works showed me that certain constellations which I could not find on the street could nonetheless be organized and arranged. And so new possibilities arise for my painting. I like videos a lot, but I must say that painting is many times more intimate. You can feel that the painted picture has passed through all the senses and not through a machine. I was in Italy and I wanted above all to see the *Visitation* of Jacopo da Pontormo in Florence. Before that I visited the Biennale in Venice. There I saw a big video on the same subject by Bill Viola. I liked it, but when I had seen it ten times I had done with it. But I am certain I could still look at Pontormo's picture in 100 years and get something out of it.

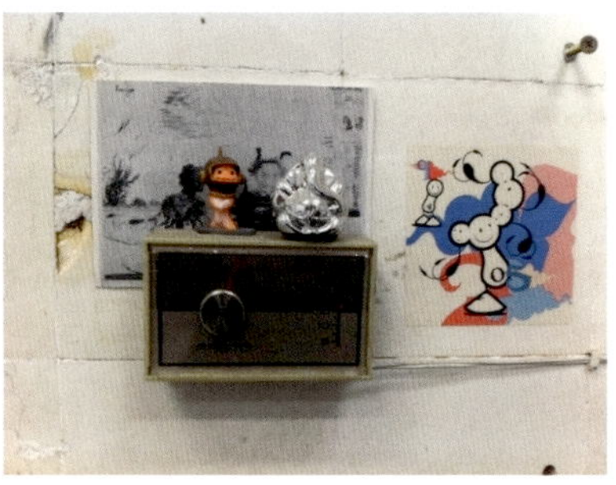

The film De zachte Weg shows six judo wrestlers on a grid square. And there are pictures by you which could be stills from the film. Did you produce the film?

Yes, I had a script and I worked through it. What interested me was the relationships between the figures and how they moved. After the film I painted the pictures; the light is the light of late morning with strong cast shadows. I think it was an important work for me.

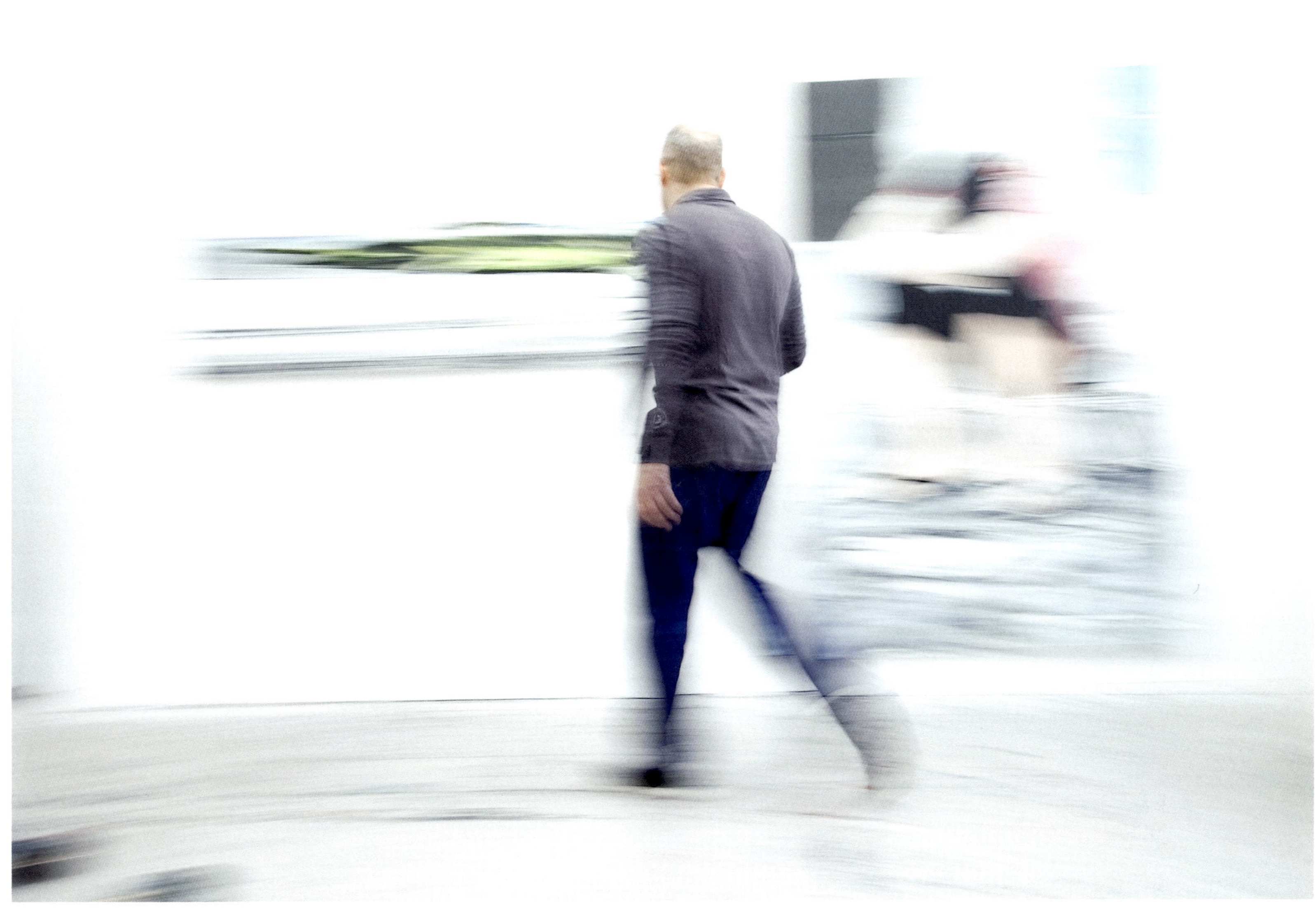

Glasshouse, 2008
200*300 cm, Öl und Acryl auf Leinwand

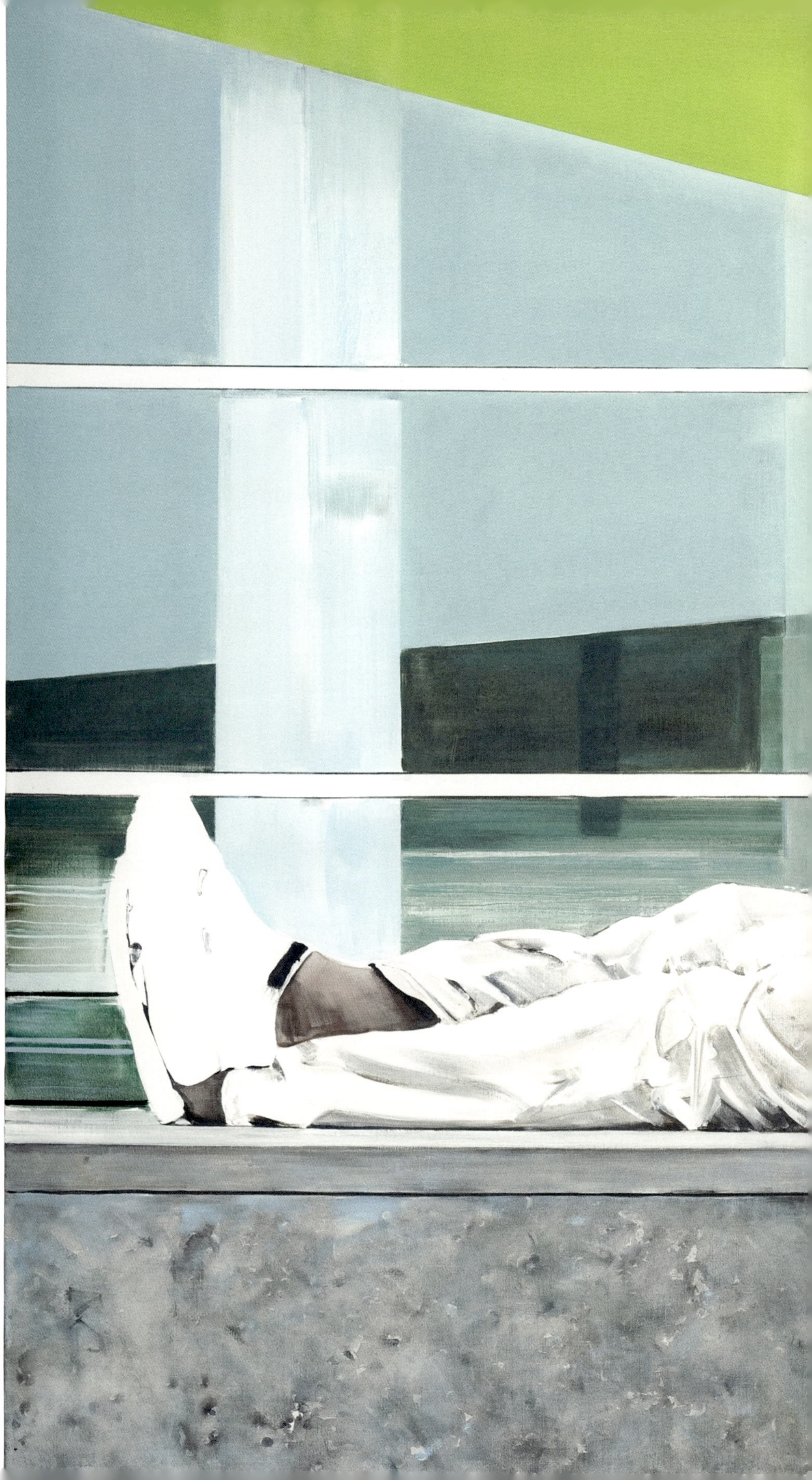

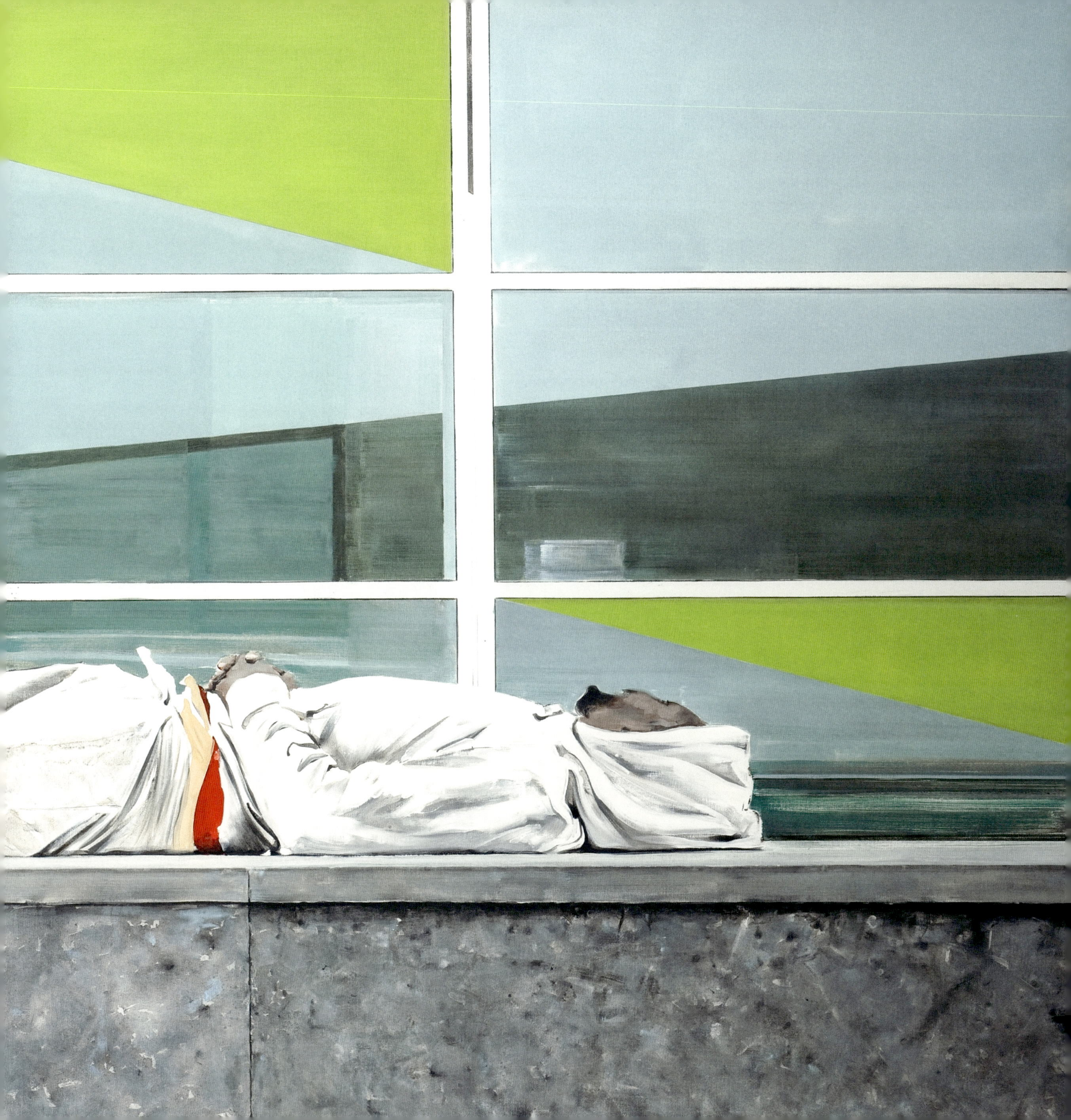

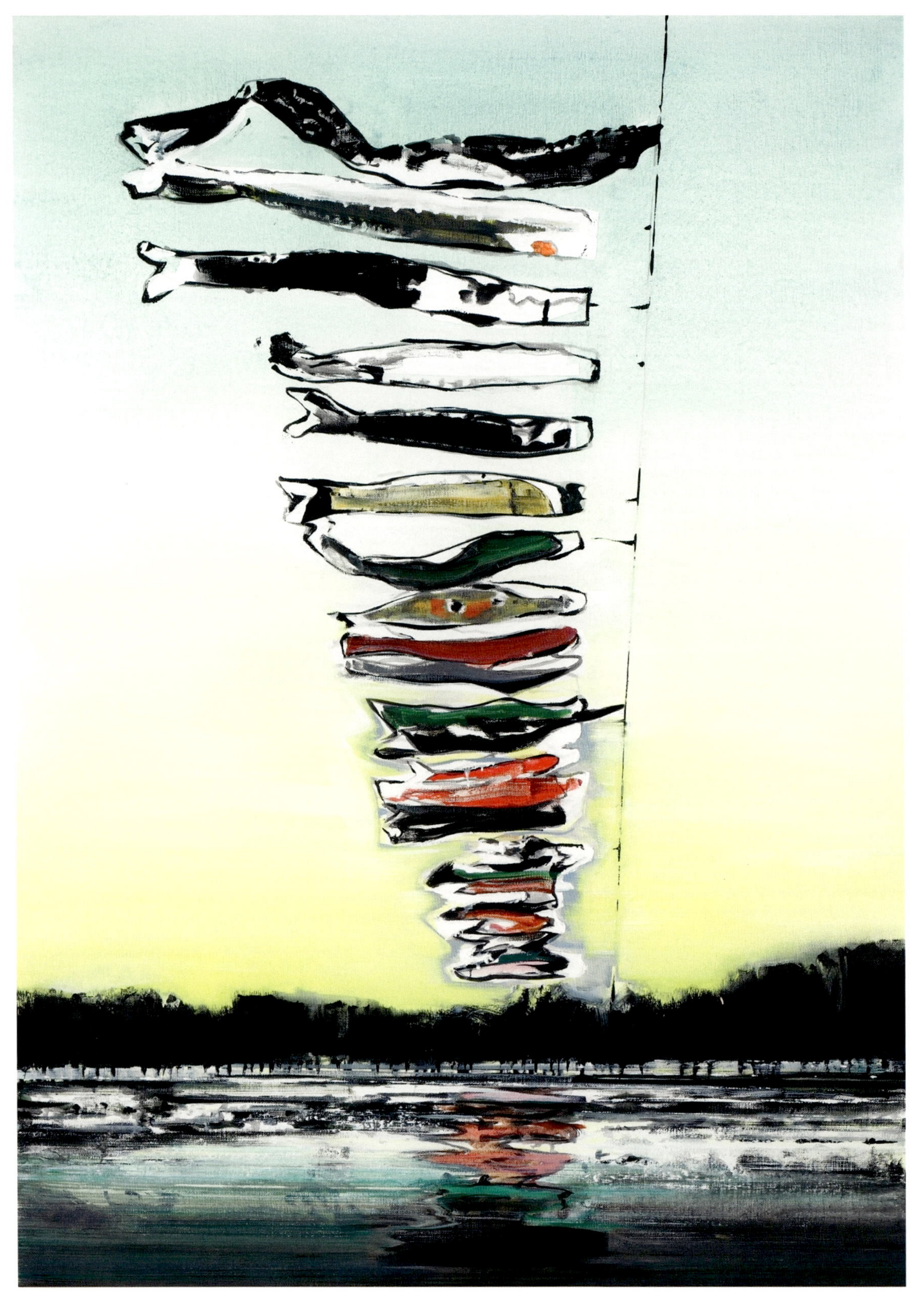

◄ *Tango No Sekku, 2007*
145*105 cm, Öl und Acryl auf Leinwand

5.oo pm, 2004 ►
200*270 cm, Öl auf Leinwand

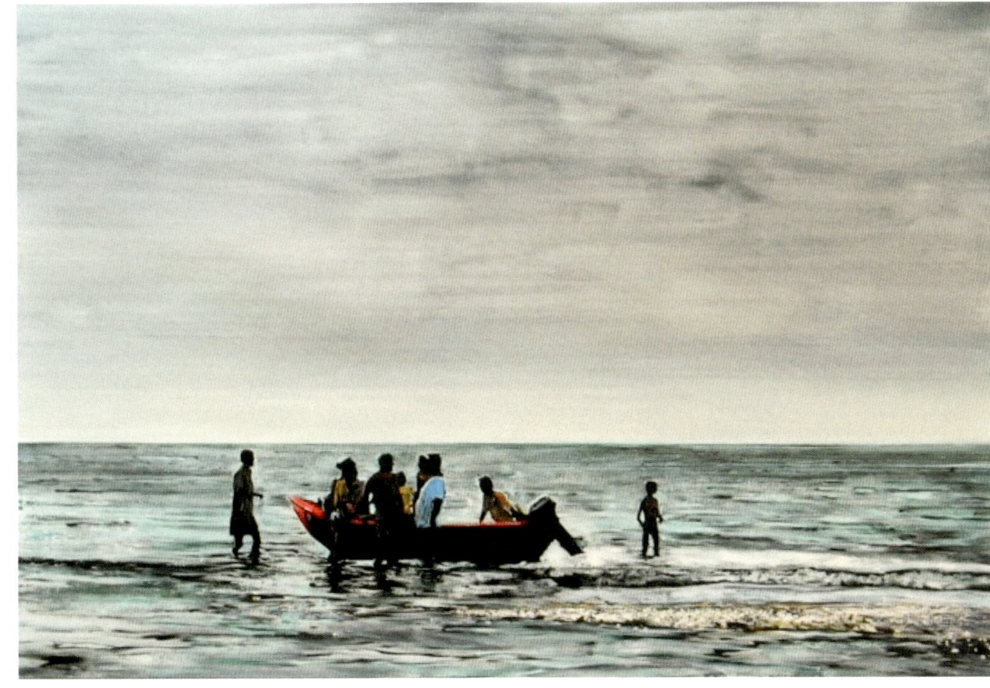

Wicky, 2007
71,4*42,2 cm, Gouache auf Papier

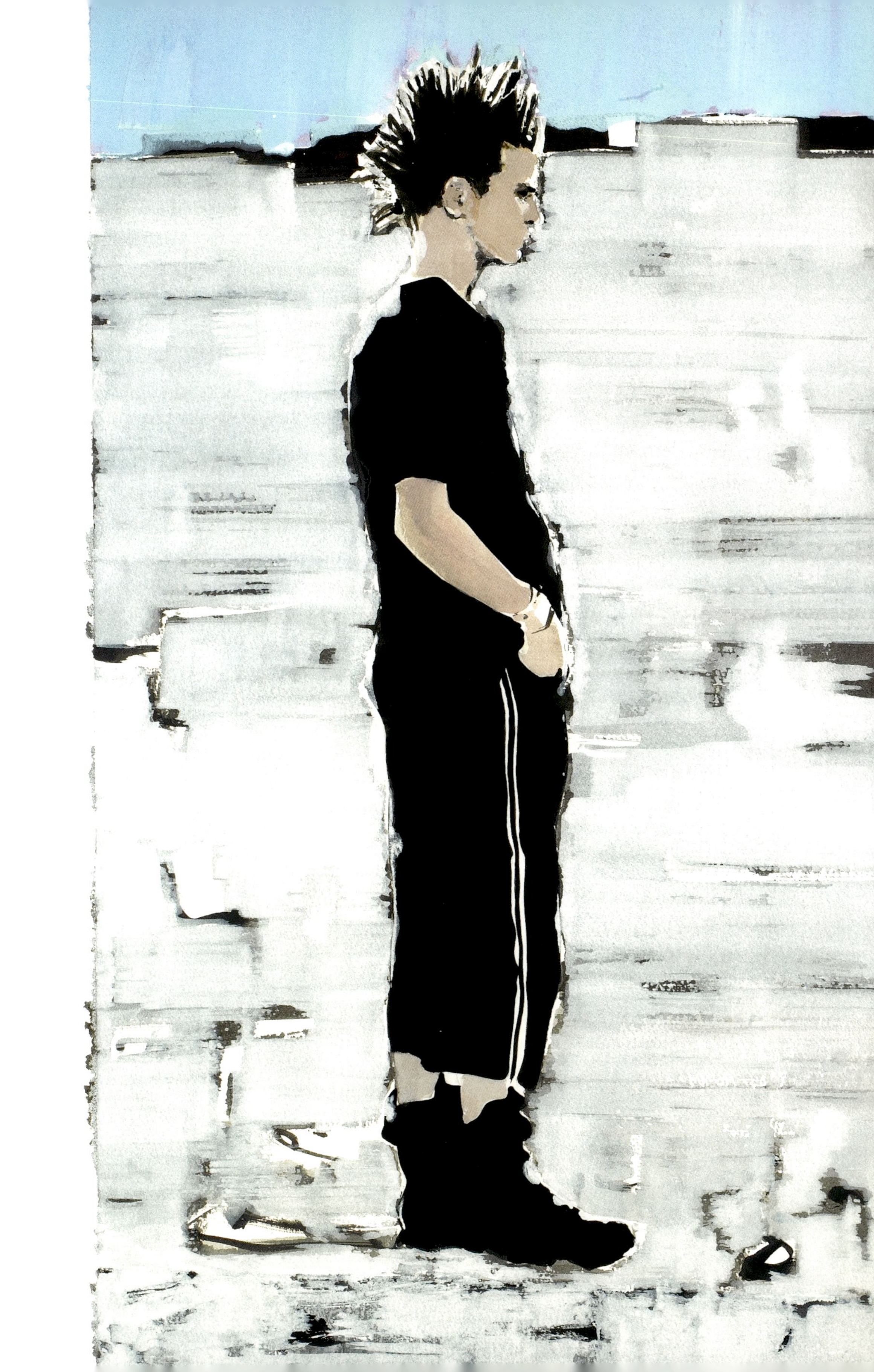

Freeze 1, 2007
145*105 cm, Öl und Acryl auf Leinwand

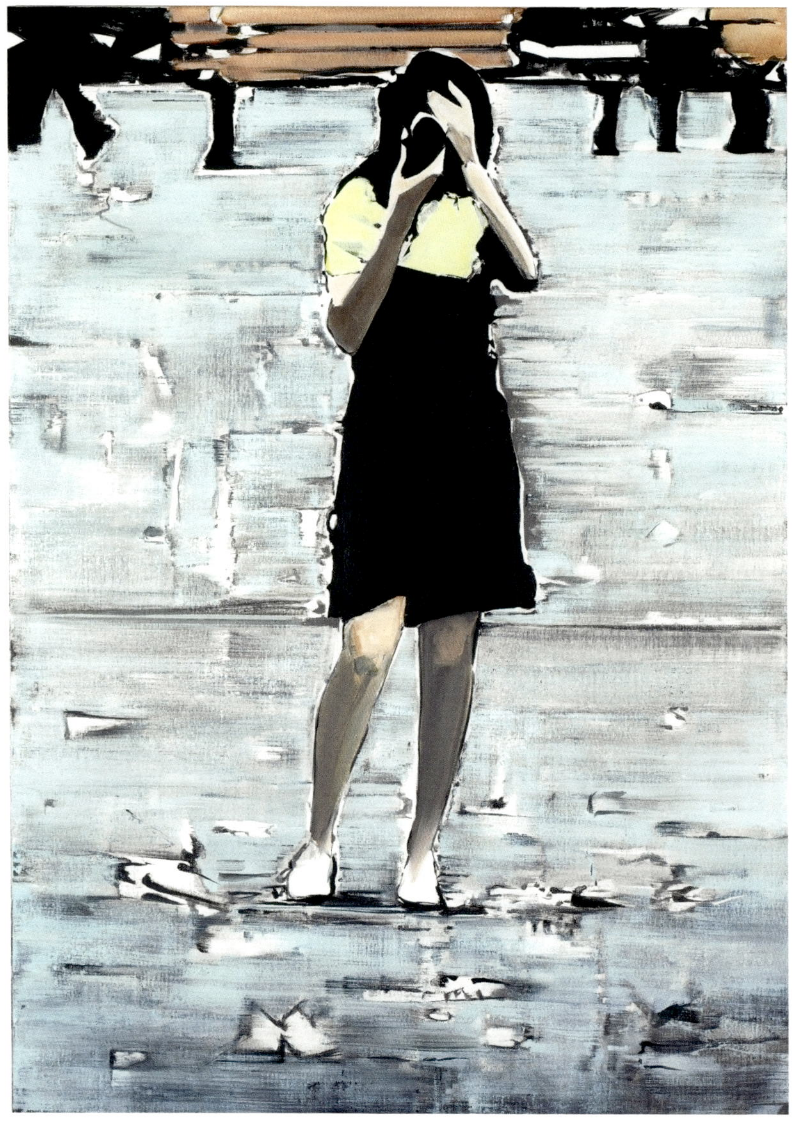

Spinning, 2005
210*200 cm, Öl und Acryl auf Leinwand

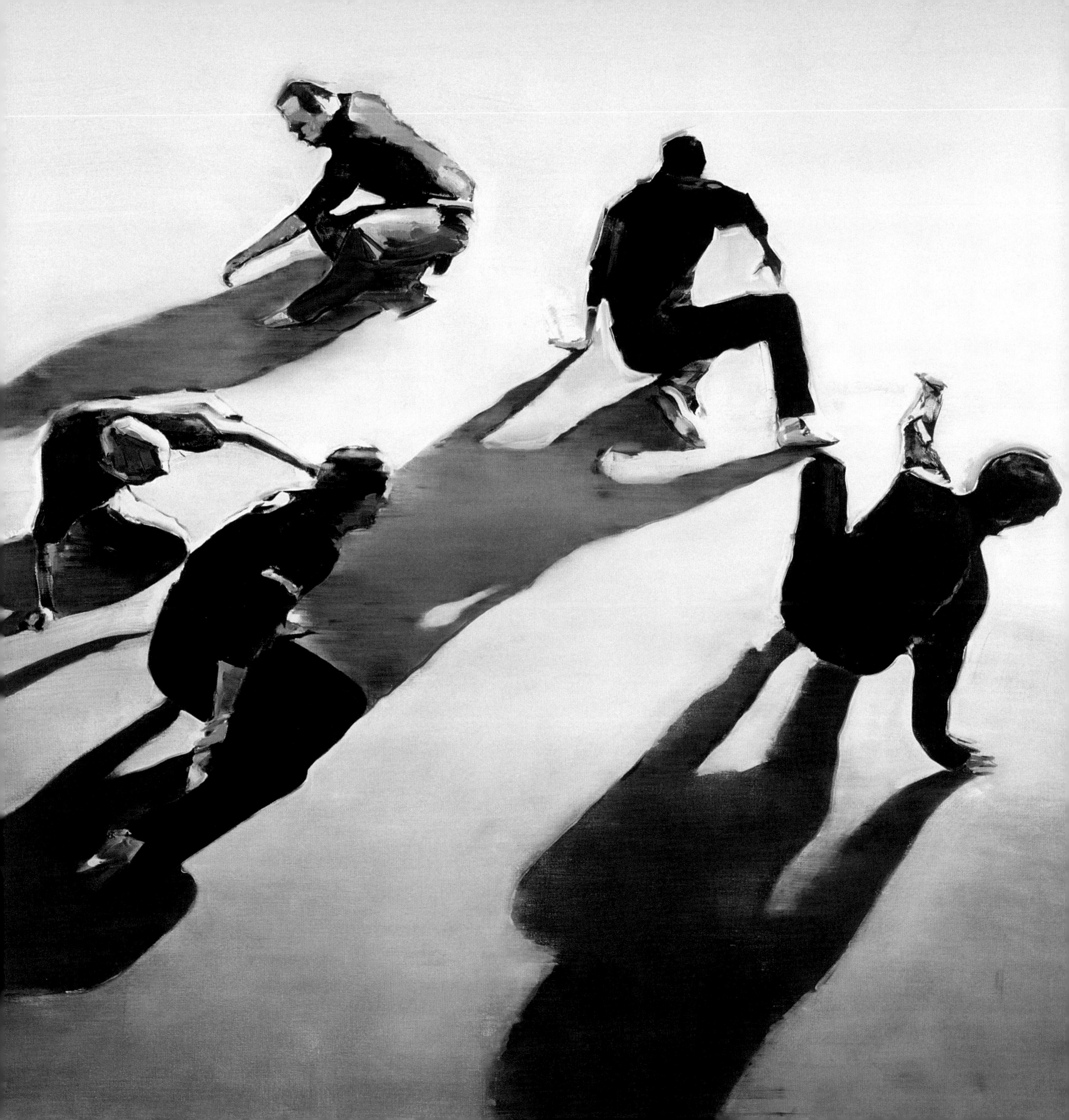

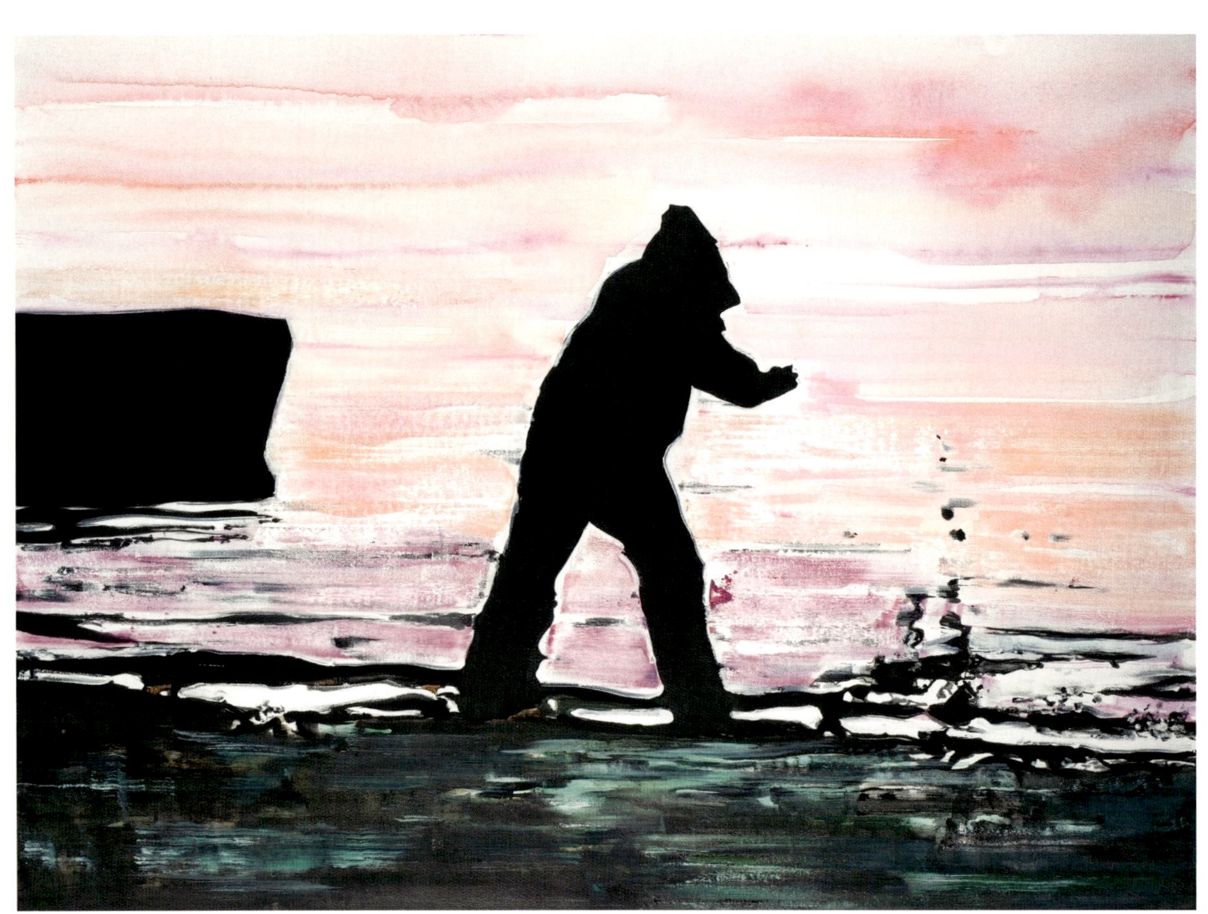

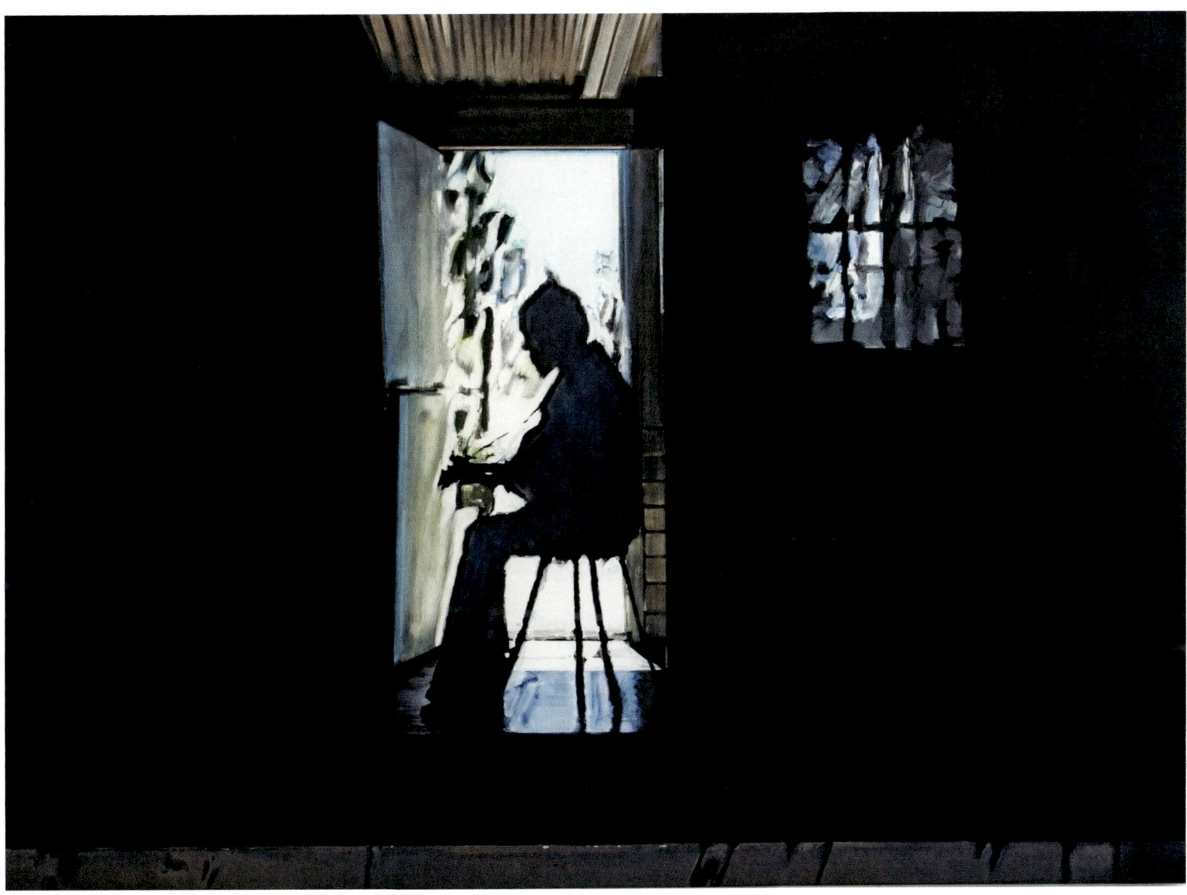

◄ **Magician, 2007**
105*145 cm, Öl und Acryl auf Leinwand

The Poet Playing, 2010 ►
190*270 cm, Öl und Acryl auf Leinwand

The Call, 2008
200*300 cm, Öl und Acryl auf Leinwand

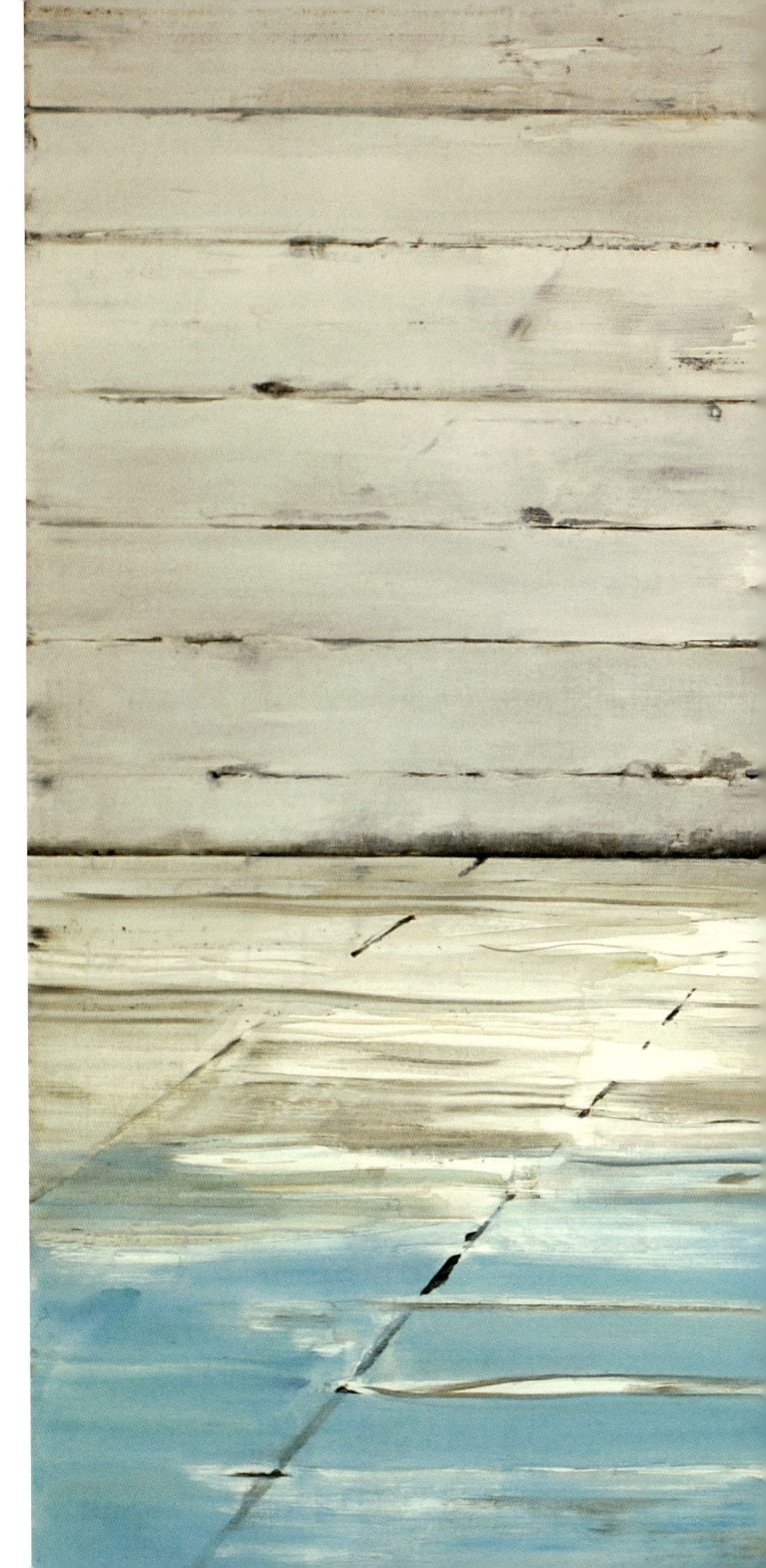

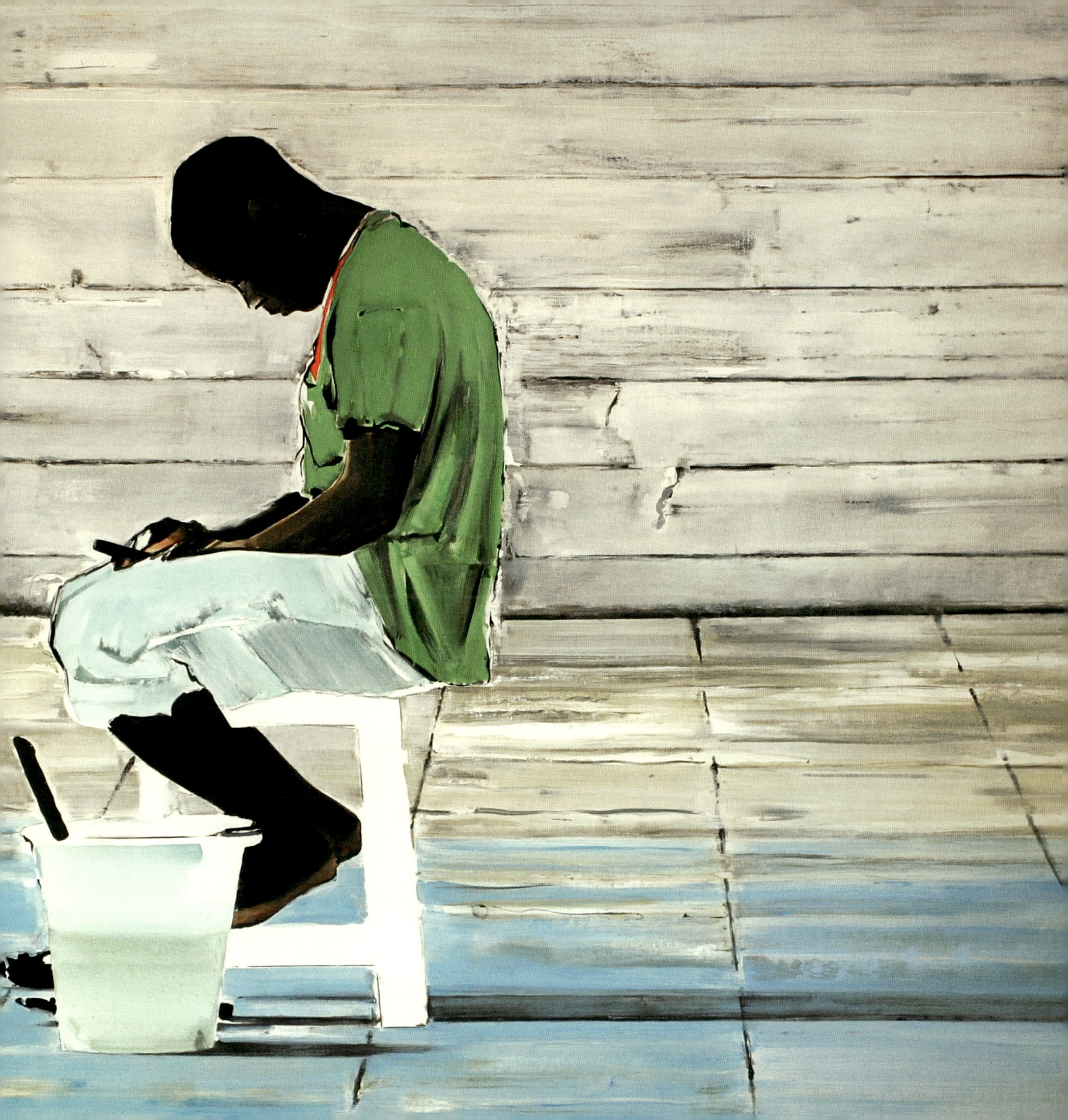

Walk in Silence

Christoph Tannert

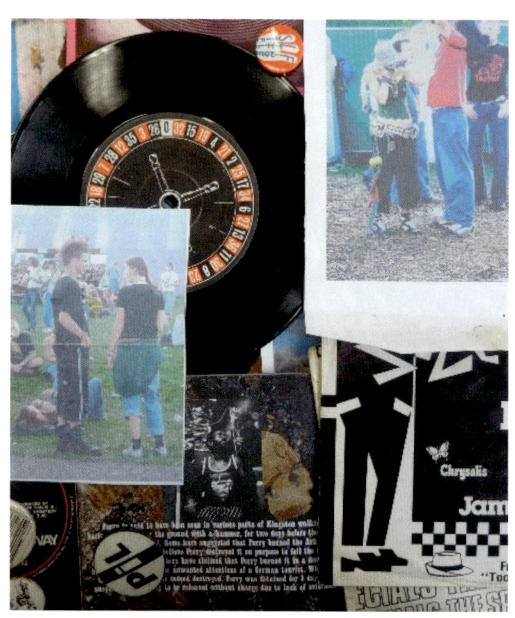

Der erste Eindruck: Lautlosigkeit in einem stillgestellten Zeitsegment.
Seine Bilder sind wie ein riesiger Warteraum, den er jeden Tag aufs Neue betritt, zeitlebens durch eine andere Tür. Im Gegensatz zu einer Welt, die uns mit Macht und Tempo überrollt, sind Vermeules Figuren ganz bei sich – stehen, schauen, ruhen aus, schlafen.
„Kairos, der glückliche Augenblick, braucht das Warten im Rücken: die manchmal quälende, manchmal selig vertrödelte, die, wie auch immer, geschenkte Zeit", verteidigt Andrea Köhler unser Recht auf „Lange Weile". [1] Sogar in Räumen, in denen sich gewöhnlich die Sprachmelodien zu einem geräuschstarken Klangteppich mischen, herrscht bei Vermeule Ruhe. Vertrödelte Tage können sich zauberhaft anfühlen, selbst wenn sie langweilig sind.

In ihrem Stillepotenzial ähneln die Bilder des Malers aus Amsterdam den schallgedämpften Romanen von Haruki Murakami, dessen Gestalten eine verwandte Aura der Einsamkeit umgibt. Würden wir Rückschlüsse auf die Gestimmtheit unserer Epoche ziehen, müssten wir aufhören, uns zu beschwichtigen und zugeben, dass wir alle Bewohner einer Endstation sind, die unsere Geduld trainiert. Murakamis Ton pathetischer Lakonie fügt sich passgenau zur postmodernen Beiläufigkeit, in der Vermeule seine Bildprotagonisten wahrnimmt. Von Bild zu Bild vergeht die Zeit und lässt sich nicht festhalten. Sie wird umschlossen von einem Kältestrom, der undurchlässig ist für die Romanhelden Murakamis, bei Vermeule aber immerhin mittels romantischer Uferlandschaften wohltemperiert oder gar neutralisiert wird.

Meist befindet sich Vermeules Bildpersonal in einem Zustand des eingeübten Wartens. Insofern geht es auch um Zeit, unsere Lebenszeit, und darum, wie wir sie verbringen. Dabei hat man nicht den Eindruck, die jungen Leute, die von Vermeule ins Blickfeld geholt werden, würden sich langweilen oder das Warten als eine Zumutung empfinden. Sie überlassen sich dem Nagen der Zeit und verbringen ihre Zeit mit dem, was man heute so tut: Abhängen, Chillen, Telefonieren (wie in *Global Nomad I*, 2008), E-Mails checken (wie in *The Call*, 2008 oder *Island*, 2011). Der zunehmenden Kurzatmigkeit unserer Existenz stellt Koen Vermeule wunderbar entspannte Bilder gegenüber, die vom gelösten Umgang mit den neuen Kommunikationsmitteln handeln und von den kleinen Kreativpausen des Alltags. Das Vertieftsein der jungen Zeitgenossen in die Nachrichten auf ihren Displays oder auch das Brieflesen eines Mannes in *The Letter* (2008) haben eine vergleichbare Intensität wie sie z.B. aus dem Klassiker des *Brieflesenden Mädchens* von Johannes Vermeer[2] spricht. Wobei Vermeule dem Verstreichen der Zeit mit Leichtigkeit gegenübertritt und den technischen Neuerungen keine überdimensionale Bedeutung zubilligt.
Sicherlich, die Welt hat sich zwischenzeitlich mehrfach gedreht, aber Koen Vermeule nutzt die Aufnahme der Verbindung zu den kunstgeschichtlichen Vorbildern, um zu unterstreichen, dass der Mensch nach wie vor nach existenziellen Bezugspunkten sucht und Pausenzeichen in seinem Leben benötigt, Konzentration. Vermeule weiß, in welcher Traditi-

The first impression is of soundlessness in a segment of time that has been laid silent. His pictures are like a vast waiting room which he re-enters every day anew, through a different door each time – all his life long. In contrast to a world that overwhelms us with its violence and speed, Koen Vermeule's figures are in harmony with themselves as they stand, watch, rest, sleep.
"Kairos, the right moment, needs the concept of hovering behind it: the time which is sometimes agony, sometimes happily dawdled away, sometimes spent in one way or another," is how Andrea Köhler defends our right to "hours of idleness." [1] Even in spaces in which the melodies of language usually become woven together into a noisy background of sounds, in Vermeule's works there is peace and quiet. Days spent in indolence can feel wonderful, even when they are monotonous.

In their potential for silence, the pictures by the artist from Amsterdam resemble the soundproofed novels of Haruki Murakami, whose characters are surrounded by a similar aura of solitude. If we were to draw conclusions about the mood of our age, we would have to stop lulling ourselves and admit that we are all inhabitants of a terminus that tests our patience.

Murakami's laconically emotive style matches precisely the postmodern casualness with which Vermeule perceives the protagonists of his pictures. From picture to picture, time passes and cannot be pinned down; it is enveloped by a chilly stream that is impene-

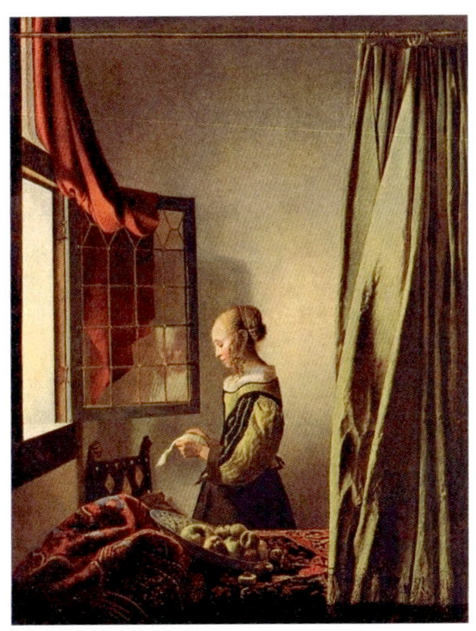

▲ ***Vermeer van Delft, Brieflesendes Mädchen am offenen Fenster, um 1657***
83*64,5 cm, Öl auf Leinwand.
Staatliche Kunstsammlungen Dresden

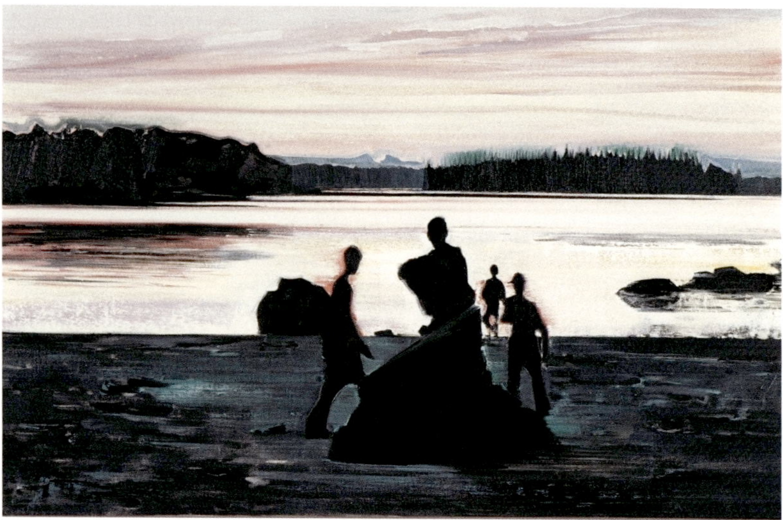

High above ground, 2003
90*140 cm, Öl und Acryl auf Leinwand

onslinie er sich befindet, deshalb hat er es nicht nötig, die Form nachzuahmen. Im Wesentlichen bemüht er sich um die der Form zugrundeliegende geistige Fassung, die er auf seine Weise und mit ausgereifter Sensorik und eigenem formalen Gepäck ins Heute transponiert. Vermeule beherrscht das gut strukturierte Spiel zwischen der leisen, zurückgenommenen figürlichen Haltung und der ungemein sinnlichen Konkretisierung der Farboberfläche. Die sensorische Breite seiner Bilder wirkt erfrischend natürlich und komplex.

Vermeule reist gern – durch die Geschichte der Bilder, durch Daseinsnischen, durch die Welt, die er in ständiger Verwandlung sieht, nie als gesicherte Existenzform. Begleitet werden Vermeules Figurenbilder von Landschaften, die in Abschirmung von weltlicher Geschwindigkeit den Schlag der Zeit verstummen lassen. Alle Sinne werden eins in diesen zum Horizont auslaufenden, endlosen Feldwegen oder den sanft ins Natürliche einschwingenden Ufer- und Strandzonen.

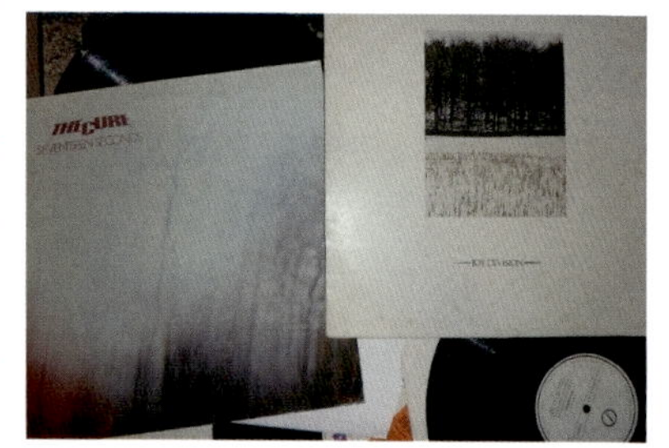

trable for the protagonists of Murakami's novels, but which for Vermeule is tempered or even neutralized by romantic shores.

The characters in Vermeule's pictures are usually in a state of practiced waiting. In that respect the subject of the pictures is time, our lifetime and how we spend it. We do not have the impression, however, that the young people on whom Vermeule focuses our attention are bored or experience the waiting as an imposition. They abandon themselves to the implacable passage of time and spend it doing what people nowadays do in such situations: hanging around, chilling out, making phone calls (as in *Global Nomad I*, 2008), or checking their e-mails (as in *The Call*, 2008 or *Island*, 2011). Koen Vermeule contrasts the increasing breathlessness of our existence with wonderfully relaxed pictures which tell of a laid-back approach to the new forms of communication and of short creative breaks in the daily routine. The absorption of our young contemporaries in the news on their displays or the way the man is reading a letter in *The Letter* (2008) display an intensity similar, for example, to the classic portrait of a *Girl Reading a Letter* by Johannes Vermeer[2]. Whereby Vermeule encounters the passage of time with lightness and does not ascribe a monumental importance to the technological innovations.
Of course the world has continued to turn steadily in the meantime, but Koen Vermeule uses the establishment of the link to his models in art history to underline the fact that people continue to search for existential points of reference and that they still need breaks in their lives, their concentration. Vermeule knows which line of tradition he is following, and so he does not need to imitate the form. In essence he is searching for the emotional state that determines the form, which he transposes into the present day in his own manner and with mature sensors and a certain amount of formal baggage. Vermeule is a master of the carefully structured interplay between the quiet, understated figurative approach and the incredibly sensuous concretization of the colored surface. The sensory spectrum of his pictures appears refreshingly natural and complex.

Vermeule likes to travel – through the history of pictures; through niches of existence; through the world, which he sees as constantly changing, but never as a secured form of existence. Vermeule's pictures of people are accompanied by landscapes that are sheltered from the pace of worldly life and where the passage of time is of no import. All the senses are united in these endless country footpaths which lead away into the distance, or the shores and beaches which extend gently into naturalness. The best, the most moving aspect of these expeditions through variously colored layers of earth and scree, plowed furrows and sand, across wastelands and pebble beaches is not only that they abandon themselves to the alternation of physical materiality without becoming brutal in their relief or cloying in their tonal harmony. It is also the tension between a genuine desire to speak up and the doubt

Das Schöne und Bewegende an diesen Expeditionen durch verschiedenfarbige Erd- und Geröllschichten, Ackerfurchen und Sand, über Brachflächen und steinige Strände hinweg ist nicht nur, dass sie sich dem Wechsel der materiellen Stofflichkeit hingeben, ohne im Relief brutal und in der tonalen Abstimmung süßlich zu werden. Es ist auch die Spannung zwischen aufrichtigem Sprechenwollen und dem Zweifel, ob durch die Mittel der Malerei überhaupt darstellbar ist, worüber man sich mitteilen möchte. In dieser stets zurückgenommenen Emphase, die sich von den auftrumpfenden Durchbrüchen zeitgenössischer europäischer Realisten merklich unterscheidet, zieht der Künstler die Grenzen der Kunst enger als die Grenzen des Mitteilungsbedürfnisses.

Vermeule gelingt es, seine ironiefreie Skepsis vor allem durch feinste Abstufungen in Lichtgebung und Dunkelapparat darzustellen. Ein kleines Bild wie *High above ground* (Abb. S. 28) ist ein Gänsehaut-Crescendo der Anteilnahme, aber ebenso das Zurückscheuen vor dem dick aufgetragenen Caspar-David-Friedrich-Gefühl und dem popistischen Glanz.
Der Habitus des Zögerns und Tastens, zuweilen auch eine melancholische Grundstimmung, kombiniert mit rissigen, malerisch ruppigen Oberflächen, leitet sich nach meiner Auffassung ab von Erfahrungen, die Koen Vermeule in den 1980er Jahren mit den radikalen Umbrüchen in der Rockmusik, mit Punk, New Wave und Ska machen konnte. Es gibt in Vermeules Werk nicht wenige Bilder, die direkt mit Bands, Songs und Texten dieser Zeit im Zusammenhang stehen, stimuliert von einer jugendlichen Verlorenheit und einem Weltschmerz, die den Kern jedes guten Rocksongs ausmachen. Ich neige dazu, Koen Vermeules Werkproduktion als ein Konzeptalbum zu sehen, das sich im Sinne einer Staffelstabübergabe entwickelt, gebettet in einen Grundton, der die Gnadenlosigkeit von Zeit und Vergänglichkeit klaglos hinnimmt.

Wenn man Koen Vermeule ein Stück näher kommen will, genügt die einfache Bildbetrachtung nicht mehr, dann muss man den Maler in seinem Kontext beschreiben. Popmusik ist sein Paralleluniversum. Im Sog aus vergangenen Klängen baut sich Vermeule eigene Loop-Schleifen und Drones im Keilrahmengeviert. Akustische Rückstände vergangener Epochen, die keine Ruhe zu finden scheinen, darunter kulturmixende Ska-, Reggae- und Calypso-Nummern über Heimweh, Leben, Tod und Statusfragen bilden eine Klangwolke, die das Künstleratelier durchzieht. Gerade läuft in seinem CD-Player ein Sampler mit Trinidadian Calypso in London (1950–1956) im Dauerbetrieb.

Die erste Platte, die Vermeule sich überhaupt gekauft hat, war das 1980 erschienene Debüt-Album der Vorreiter des Ska-Revivals The Specials, das mit Sicherheit zu den wichtigsten 100 Platten des 20. Jahrhunderts gezählt werden wird. Zuspätgekommenen sind Mitglieder der Band vermutlich bekannt durch Specials-Coverversionen von Amy Winehouse und einen Auftritt, den sie 2009 zusammen mit Winehouse auf dem britischen „V-Festival" in

as to whether it is even possible to represent what one wants to say via the medium of painting. In this invariably understated emphasis, which is far removed from the boastful breakthroughs of contemporary European Realists, the artist draws the boundaries of art more tightly than the boundaries of the need to communicate.

Vermeule succeeds in depicting his skepticism, which is devoid of irony, primarily through the fine nuances of the lighting and shadows. A small picture like *High above ground* (fig. p. 28) is a crescendo of sympathy which gives viewers the shivers while at the same time making them shy away from the Caspar David Friedrich-feeling and the Popist splendor that Vermeule applies thickly.
In my view the habitual hesitancy and groping, and the occasional melancholy overall mood combined with cracked, rough, painterly surfaces, is derived from the experiences which Koen Vermeule had in the nineteen-eighties with the radical changes in rock music, with punk, new wave and ska. In Vermeule's oeuvre there are quite a number of pictures that are directly connected to bands, songs, and texts of this period, stimulated by the youthful forlornness and *Weltschmerz* which form the core of every good rock song. I tend to see Koen Vermeule's production of artworks as a concept album which develops like the handing over of a relay baton, embedded in a keynote which uncomplainingly accepts the mercilessness of time and transience.

If one wants to get to know Koen Vermeule and his work better, it will no longer be sufficient merely to look at his pictures; it will be necessary to describe the artist in his context. Pop music is his parallel universe. In the undertow of past sounds, Vermeule constructs his own loops and drones within the rectangle of his stretcher frame. Acoustic remnants of past eras which seem not to come to rest, including numbers about homesickness, life, death, and questions of status mix the cultures of ska, reggae, and calypso and form a cloud of sound which permeates the artist's studio. At the moment a sampler with Trinidadian calypso in London (1950–1956) is playing non-stop on his CD player.

The first record which Vermeule bought himself was the debut album by The Specials – the forerunners of the ska revival – wich appeared in 1980 and which is certain to be included in a list of the one hundred most important records during the twentieth century. Those who arrived on the scene too late will probably know members of the band from the Specials cover versions by Amy Winehouse and an appearance they made in 2009 together with Winehouse at the British V-Festival in Chelmsford. Looking back, Diederich Diederichsen speaks of the experience of an entire generation in East and West which was shaped by counter-culture when he admits: "For the first time it was music full of anger which was not so clumsy that it photographed protest and anger directly, but rather recorded it

Chelmsford hatten. Diedrich Diederichsen spricht rückblickend die gegenkulturell geprägte Erfahrung einer ganzen Generation in Ost und West an, wenn er bekennt: „Das war zum ersten Mal Wut-Musik, die nicht so plump war, Aufschrei und Wut direkt abfotografieren zu müssen, sie vielmehr in stilisierter Bewegung symbolisch festhielt, ohne ihre Energie zu verlieren (eine alte Tugend schwarzer Musik)." [3] Mit vier Top-Ten-Hits sind die Specials im England der 1980er Jahre Stars. Ihre Platten erscheinen auf dem von Keyboarder Jerry Dammers gegründeten Label „2-Tone", das damals als das heißeste Indie-Label auf der Insel gilt und in der Gründungsphase auch Madness, The Beat (UK) und The Selecter unter Vertrag hat. 2-Tone tritt strikt antirassistisch in Erscheinung. Die Specials sind eine gemischte Combo. Symbol dieser Ausrichtung ist das bis heute Anwendung findende Schachbrettmuster. Zum größten Erfolg der Band wird die Single *Ghost Town,* die im Sommer 1981 erscheint, zeitgleich zu den Aufständen in Brixton und Liverpool, und Massenarbeitslosigkeit und alltäglichen Rassismus im Vereinigten Königreich glaubhaft zur Sprache bringt. Obwohl die BBC den Song indiziert, belegt er Platz 1 der Charts und avanciert zu einer künstlerisch gelungenen Revoluzzer-Hymne mit leicht schmalzigem Krisen-Feeling. Unter Ost-Berlins Bedingungen der Schattenwirtschaft ist die LP Kult bei denen, die einen besseren Sozialismus erträumen – und kostet 100 DDR-Mark oder mehr.

Vermeules Lieblingssong ist das *Doesn't make it allright,* ein langsamer, rocksteadymäßig federnder Ska, der mit der aufmunternden Zeile beginnt: „Just because you're nobody. It doesn't mean that you're no good ..." [4] Die spätere, aggressivere Version der Stiff Little Fingers, die die erlebte Revolte mitdenkt, radikalisiert das Ich und begeistert Vermeule gleichermaßen.

Koen Vermeule, daran interessiert, der Sprachlosigkeit im politischen Prozess zu entkommen, schätzt auch andere Bands dieses Jahrzehnts aus dem Sammelbecken all jener disparaten Motive, die in der nur scheinbar homogenen Punk-Protestbewegung aufeinandertreffen. Zu seiner musikalischen Mitte als mitdenkender Fan gehört der früh verstorbene Sänger Jeffrey Lee Pierce von The Gun Club. Wichtig für ihn werden darüber hinaus das erste Album der Ramones, das sämtliche Staudämme der Musikwelt zum Brechen brachte, was längst fällig war, und die brutale Authentizität von The Clash, besonders das rohe, chaosstiftende *Police and Thieves* (von 1977). Erst später entdeckt er die dazugehörige Vorläufer-Version (von 1976), einen Radau-Reggae über Gang-Unwesen und Polizeigewalt, geschrieben von Junior Murvin, dem früheren Gitarristen von Bob Marley & The Wailers, produziert von Lee Perry. In Jamaika war der Song einer der größten Hits des Dezenniums. [5]

Im Jahr 2003, während eines Urlaubs in Schweden, zeltet Vermeule an einem entzückend gelegenen See. An einem Abend kreuzen ein paar junge Leute auf. Um den Moment der Begegnung festzuhalten, die den Künstler anhaltend euphorisiert, schießt Vermeule ein paar Fotos,

symbolically in stylized movement without losing its energy (an old virtue of black music)." [3] With four Top-Ten hits, the Specials were stars in the England of the nineteen-eighties. Their records appeared on the label 2-Tone, founded by keyboard player Jerry Dammers. It was regarded as the hottest indie label on the island and in the founding phase also had contracts with Madness, The Beat (UK), and The Selecter. 2-Tone was strictly anti-racist and The Specials were a mixed combo. The symbol for this orientation remains the checkerboard pattern which is still in use to this day. The band's biggest hit was the single "Ghost Town", which appeared in the summer of 1981 at the same time as the riots in Brixton and Liverpool, debating in a convincing manner the subjects of mass unemployment and everyday racism within the United Kingdom. Although the BBC indexed the song it occupied the top position in the charts and became an artistically successful revolutionary hymn with its slightly schmaltzy crisis feeling. Under the informal economy conditions that prevailed in East Berlin, the LP became a cult object among those who dreamed of a better type of socialism – and cost 100 DDR marks or more.

Vermeule's favorite song was *"Doesn't Make it Allright"*, a slow, rock-steady type of bouncy ska which starts with the encouraging line: "Just because you're nobody. It doesn't mean that you're no good ..." [4] Vermeule was equally enthusiastic about the later, more aggressive version by Stiff Little Fingers, which followed the revolt which had taken place and radicalized the individual.

Koen Vermeule was interested in escaping the voicelessness of the political process and also valued other bands of the decade from the melting pot of all the widely differing motives which joined together in the punk protest movement but which only superficially had elements in common.

His musical focus as a fan with a mind of his own included the singer Jeffrey Lee Pierce of The Gun Club, who died at an early age. Also important for him was the first album by the Ramones, which released the pent-up energy of the music world, long overdue, and the brutal authenticity of The Clash, especially the raw, anarchic *"Police and Thieves"* (of 1977). It was only later that he discovered the associated earlier version (of 1976), an unbridled reggae about gang troublemaking and police violence, written by Junior Murvin, the earlier guitarist of Bob Marley & The Wailers and produced by Lee Perry. In Jamaica the song was one of the biggest hits of the decade. [5]

During a holiday in Sweden in 2003, Vermeule was camping beside a charming lake. One evening a group of young people appeared. In order to record the moment of encounter, which aroused a long-lasting mood of euphoria in the artist, Vermeule took a few photos. He did not simply call the picture, which he produced at a later date, *"Summer Night with Friends,"* but *High above ground* (fig. p. 28). [6] He borrowed the title from the song *"Hanging*

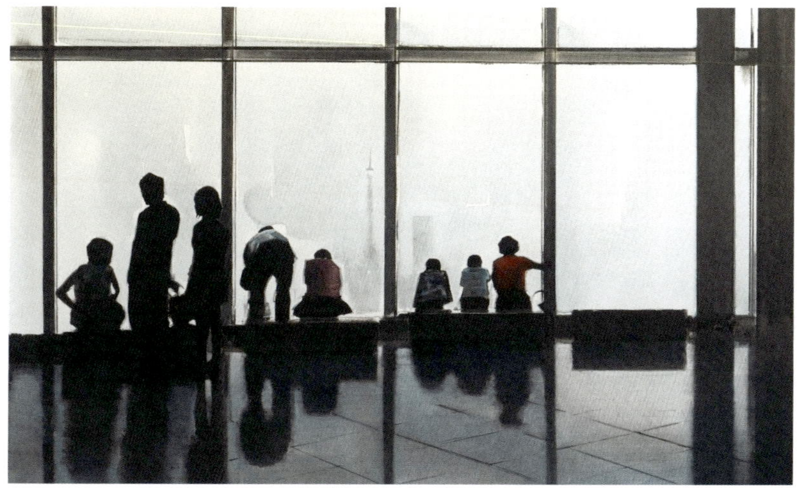

***Top of the World*, 2011**
110*180 cm, Öl und Acryl auf Leinwand

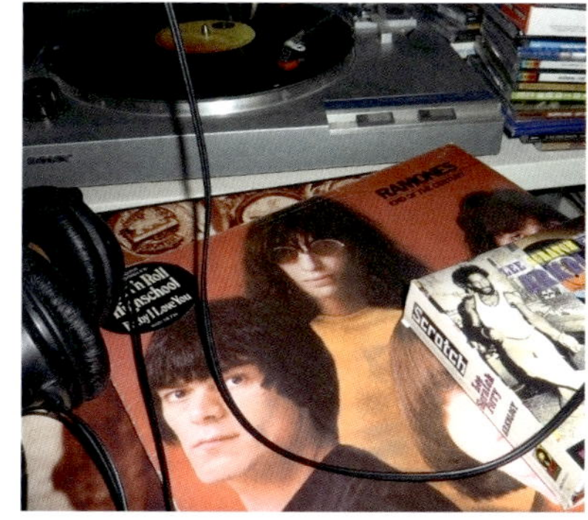

nennt das später entstandene Bild aber nicht einfach *Sommernacht mit Freunden*, sondern *High above ground* (Abb. S. 28).[6] Den Titel entlehnt er dem Song *Hanging around* der Band The Stranglers. Jugenderinnerungen und eine ganz gegenwärtige Introspektion über Sinnsuche und Lebenserfüllung treffen sich in einem Erzählraum, der konkretisiert wird durch einen Entschleunigungsakzent. Am emotionalen Fixpunkt nehmen wir die stilsichere Tristesse der Stranglers als Klangmalerei wahr. Bis zur Auflösung der Band 1990 sammelt Vermeule sämtliche ihrer LPs und Singles.

Seine Anteilnahme an den realen Aktionen und dem Modus der ausgependelten Tage der jungen Generation von heute findet ablesbaren Niederschlag in farbsatten Bildern. Der Künstler registriert den Protest gegen den Stand der Dinge. Er malt Gegenwart im verinnerlichten Beat der Dissidenz, freilich ohne seine Malerei punkig aufzukitschen. Nur weil er sie bewahrt vor dick aufgetragenem Remmidemmi, ist sie überzeugend. Vor glutroter Sonnenuntergangskulisse in

around" by The Stranglers. Memories of youth and an entirely contemporary introspection about the search for meaning and the fulfillment of life meet in a narrative space which is made concrete through a mood of deceleration. At the emotional fixed point we experience the stylistic confidence of the Stranglers' tristesse as onomatopoeia. Until the band was dissolved in 1990 Vermeule collected all their LPs and singles.

His participation in the real actions and style of the aimless days of today's younger generation leaves recognizable traces in the rich colors of the pictures. The artist registers the protest against the status quo. He paints the presence in the internalized beat of dissidence, admittedly, without adding elements of kitsch to his painting in punk style. It is only convincing because he preserves it from the excesses of a rumpus. Against a fiery red sunset backdrop in *Beached* (2008), the children of wrath no longer look like the losers from the French banlieues, but rather like a crowd of relaxed beachcombers.
Those who believe that Vermeule is thereby making use of an "idolization of the juvenile," (to borrow a universally valid combat term by Carl Einstein) are much mistaken. His pictorial ideas are addressed to sixteen-year-olds of all ages. Vermeule's pictures release sounds in the inner ear and portray the antagonism between naivety and change of time interval in consciously reduced arrangements. With his finger on the pulse of time he creates miniatures, not so much hymns: densely woven webs of color, elaborate compositions, inspired in their execution.
The mild degree of unsharpness, which makes accessible new aspects and diversions in the pictures in the back of our mind's eye, arises not least in the dialogue with photographs that the artist previously collected but now tends to take himself. The photo that provided the starting point for *Morning a Cruel Turmoiler* is[7] must have been taken in about 2007 at the Lowlands Festival in Biddinghuizen. Isolated in the crowd of concert spectators, the artist encountered a supine figure that seemed to exist on a different wavelength from the generally experienced one. Vermeule has extracted the motif from a group photo. This allows us to concentrate more specifically on form and content. A mood of disillusionment is enhanced in a painterly manner so that it slides over into a sphere of meditative security which is almost identical to the one that can be comfortably experienced in the wellness areas of the Western world in general. Vermeule does not allow himself to be bound by the framework of pictorial associations. His prime concern is the protean, which considers content falling outside the everyday norm.

From time to time the scenic harmony is interrupted by a chilly draught, a frosty mood. At an early stage Vermeule was inspired to this approach to landscape by two record covers: a single by Joy Division and one by The Cure (fig. p. 28).
The single by Joy Division was first published in France in 1980 with the deliberately cho-

Beached (2008) sehen die Kinder des Zorns nicht mehr wie die Verlierer aus den französischen Vorstädten aus, eher wie ein Haufen relaxender Strandläufer.

Wer meint, Vermeule diene sich damit einer „Vergötzung des Juvenilen" an (um einen allzeit gültigen Kampfbegriff Carl Einsteins zu gebrauchen), der irrt. Seine Bildideen sind adressiert an die 16-Jährigen aller Altersklassen. Vermeules Bilder setzen Klänge im Innenohr frei und zeichnen den Antagonismus zwischen Naivität und Änderung des Zeittakts in bewusst verschlankten Arrangements. Am Puls der Zeit entstehen Miniaturen, weniger Hymnen, dicht gesponnene Farbgewebe, durchdachte Kompositionen, beseelt in ihrer Umsetzung.

Der milde Unschärfegrad, der den Bildern neue Seiten- und Umwege im Augenhintergrund zugänglich macht, kommt nicht zuletzt im Dialog mit fotografischen Bildern zustande, die der Künstler früher gesammelt hat, nun aber mehr und mehr selbst anfertigt. Die Fotovorlage von *Morning a Cruel Turmoiler is*[7] muss etwa 2007 beim „Lowlands Festival" in Biddinghuizen entstanden sein. Isoliert aus der Masse der Konzertbesucher trifft der Künstler auf eine auf dem Rücken liegende Figur, die auf einer anderen als der allgemein bekannten Wirklichkeitsfrequenz zu existieren scheint. Vermeule hat das Motiv aus einer fotografischen Gruppenaufnahme extrahiert. Das lässt uns konzentrierter über Form und Inhalt nachdenken. Malerisch aufgewertet wird eine Stimmung der Desillusion, die in eine Sphäre meditativer Geborgenheit hinübergleitet, die jener zum Verwechseln ähnlich ist, in der es sich in den Wellnessbereichen der westlichen Welt im Allgemeinen ganz kommod leben lässt. Vermeule legt sich und den bildlichen Assoziationsrahmen nicht an die Kette. Priorität hat das Vielgestaltige, das die aus der Norm fallenden Sachverhalte mitdenkt.

Zuweilen wird die landschaftliche Ausgewogenheit unterbrochen durch einen unterkühlten Zug, eine frostige Stimmung. Frühe Anstöße zu seiner Landschaftsauffassung empfing Vermeule durch zwei Schallplattenhüllen – eine Single von Joy Division und eine von The Cure (Abb. S. 28). Die Single von Joy Division wurde erstmalig 1980 in Frankreich unter dem bewusst gewählten deutschen Titel *Licht und Blindheit* veröffentlicht, um möglichst viel expressionistischen Sprengstoff zu bündeln. Sie enthielt auf der A-Seite den *Titel Atmosphere* sowie *Dead Souls* auf der B-Seite. Nach dem überraschenden Selbstmord von Sänger Ian Curtis (am 18. Mai 1980) wurde Atmosphere zusammen mit *She's Lost Control* als Double-A-sided-Single in England erneut auf den Markt gebracht. Das typografische Konzept für die Hülle verantwortete Peter Saville, dessen keilschriftartiger Minimalismus fast alle Cover von Joy Division und New Order auszeichnete und das Platten-Label Factory Records visuell unverwechselbar machte. Auf der Vorderseite der Single sieht man ein Landschaftsfoto von Charles Meecham, in kontrastreichem Schwarz-Weiß gehalten – Zweiteilung der Welt: eine Kompanie kahler Winterbäume im oberen Bildteil, unten ein räudiger Stoppelacker. Der testosteronfreie Darkwave und die harte, tiefe Stimme von Ian Curtis kanalisieren den Hilferuf aus der Kälte: „... Don't walk away in silence, Don't walk away."[8]

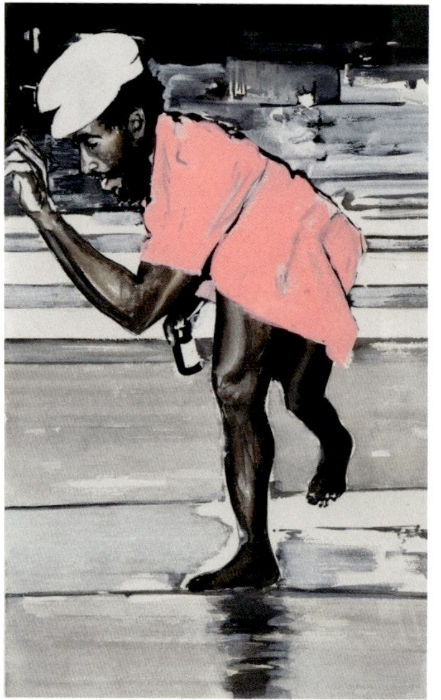

sen German title *Licht und Blindheit (Light and Blindness)*, in order to gather together as much expressionist dynamite as possible. It had the track *Atmosphere* on the A-side and *Dead Souls* on the B-side. After the unexpected suicide of singer Ian Curtis (on 18 May 1980), *Atmosphere* was marketed again in England as a double A-sided single together with *She's Lost Control*. Peter Saville was responsible for the typographical concept of the record cover; the almost minimalist cuneiform lettering was a characteristic of virtually all the covers for Joy Division and New Order and made the Factory Records label visually distinctive. On the front of the single is a landscape photo by Charles Meecham, in stark black and white contrasts.

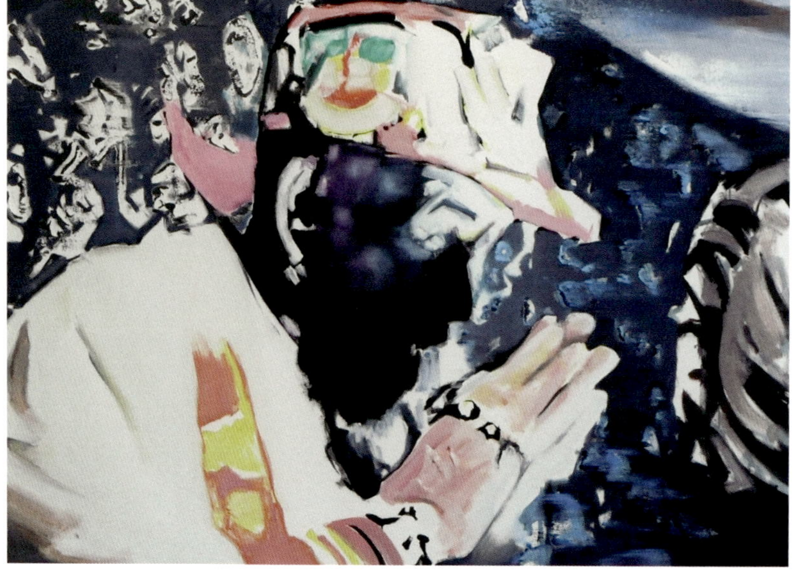

▲ **Spirit chaser, 2009**
105*145 cm, Öl und Acryl auf Leinwand

▲▲ **Pissed, 2009**
100*60 cm, Gouache auf Papier

The world is divided in two: a line of bare winter trees in the upper part of the picture, while below there is a mangy field of stubble. The testosterone-free darkwave and the hard, deep voice of Ian Curtis channel the cry for help from the cold: "... Don't walk away in silence, Don't walk away."[8]

Wie ein Song, ein Satz, ein Interieur, eine Landschaft sich zum Aufenthaltsraum für erfrorene Seelen wandelt, wie die verzweifelte Suche nach Liebe in destilliertes Erleben umgeformt wird, das muss Koen Vermeule, eingeschlossen in diesen Eisschrank, hier zum ersten Mal bewusst wahrgenommen haben.

Das Cover von *A Forest* von The Cure bedient sich ebenfalls eines Schwarz-Weiß-Fotos, vorn als Positiv, hinten als Negativ gedruckt, Motiv: verwilderter Märchenwald. Als Auskopplung aus dem zweiten Album von The Cure, *Seventeen Seconds*, 1980 erschienen, gilt *A Forest* gemeinhin als charakteristischer Cure-Song in typischer untröstlicher Weinerlichkeit, vorangetrieben von Simon Gallups munter hüpfendem Bass und Lol Tolhursts maschinenpräzisem Schlagzeug. Das Anhören solch eines Titels gleicht dem Gang auf einem zugefrorenen See, bei dem man nicht genau weiß, ob das Eis trägt. Das dazugehörige Cover ist als Zufluchtsraum gestaltet, angefüllt mit Klängen. In seinem Kopf hat Vermeule das Bild bewahrt, im Bann von The Cure und in Hingabe an Lebenslust als einziger Überlebensstrategie.

Koen Vermeule, imprisoned in this refrigerator, must have experienced here for the first time how a song, a sentence, an interior, a landscape, can be transformed into a common space for frozen souls; how the desperate search for love is transformed into distilled experience.

The cover of "A Forest" by The Cure also displays a black-and-white photo, printed on the front as a positive image and on the back as a negative. The motif is a fairy-tale forest which has gone wild. A single from The Cure's second album *Seventeen Seconds* (1980), "A Forest" is in any case regarded as a typical Cure song, its characteristic inconsolable weepiness driven forward by Simon Gallup's lively hopping bass and Lol Tolhurst's mechanically precise percussion. Listening to a song like this is like walking across a frozen lake when you are not certain whether the ice will hold. The matching cover is designed as a panic room filled with sound. Vermeule preserved the picture in his head under the spell of The Cure and in commitment to joie-de-vivre as his only survival strategy.

Egal, mit welchem Ohr er sich über die Jahre durch Zeiten und Stile hörte, nach einigen hippen Alben und allzeit ungebremster Lust am Ohrwurm landete Vermeule irgendwann bei Lee „Scratch" Perry, dem Reggae-Regenten, der mit King Tubby zusammen den Dub erfand und die Grundprinzipien des Remixens. Perry verehrt er so sehr, dass er dem Meister ein Porträt widmete: *Spirit Chaser* – Farbe im sonischen Nebel, typisches Jamming, Dröhnen, ballernder Bass, der einen zum Tanzen bringt. The Clash schrieben ihr *Police and Thieves* zusammen mit Lee Perry.

Regardless of how he listened to times and styles across the years, after a few hip albums and invariably unbridled pleasure in catchy tunes, at some point Vermeule landed with Lee "Scratch" Perry, the regent of reggae, who together with King Tubby invented the dub and the basic principles of the remix. He respected Perry so greatly that he dedicated a portrait of the master to him: Spirit Chaser – color in the sonic fog, typical jamming, a blasting, thundering bass which inspires you to get up and dance. The Clash wrote their *"Police & Thieves"* together with Lee Perry.

Die Art, wie die jungen Leute in Vermeules Bild *Beached* (2008) ihre Gegenwart im Feuer der untergehenden Sonne auskosten, sich die Zukunft ausmalen, und wie der Maler ihr Aufbegehren während der Ausschreitungen in den Pariser Vororten erlebte, hat nicht wenig miteinander zu tun. Vermeules Bilder sind eindringlicher als die üblichen Pamphlete. Sie werden den Ungerechtigkeiten in der Welt keinen Stoß versetzen, aber sie geben der Welt Farbe zurück und lassen Kunst ein Werkzeug für Inspiration und Veränderung sein. Das Konzept dieser Bilder, die Partei ergreifen für die junge Generation, ist: neugierig machen statt anklagen. Sie sind dringend notwendig. In Zeiten der Intoleranz und der Zerrbilder, die das kollektive Bewusstsein prägen, stellen sie den Blick auf die Freiheit scharf.

The way in which the young people in Vermeule's picture Beached (2008) revel in the present in the glow of the setting sun, and map out their futures is strongly related to the way in which the painter experienced their protests during the unrest in the Paris suburbs. Vermeule's pictures are more forceful than the usual pamphlets. They will not overturn the injustices in the world, but they give the world back its color and allow art to become a tool for inspiration and change. The concept of these pictures, which speak up on behalf of the younger generation, is to arouse curiosity instead of indicting. They are urgently needed. In times of intolerance and distorted pictures which leave their mark on the collective consciousness, they bring freedom into focus.

Koen Vermeule hat eine spezielle Art, verschwindende Augenblicke zu erinnern, festzuhalten und damit zu re-präsentieren. Den durch die Gegend schweifenden, zerstreuten Blick bannt er mit Einzelbildern, die man ausloten und für die man sich Zeit nehmen muss. Vermeule fixiert Seherlebnisse, die vielfach Hörerlebnisse sind, und versichert sich ihrer Präsenz. So entsteht eine Erlebniszeit, die einen neuen Raum öffnet, den wir erfahren können, der aber trotzdem seine Geheimnisse nicht vollständig preisgibt. Seine Bilder besitzen ein Streu-

Koen Vermeule has a special way of recalling fleeting moments, recording them and thus bringing them to mind once more. He catches the attention of the roaming gaze as it scans the horizon with snapshots that viewers have to sound out and for which they must take time. Vermeule focuses on visual experiences which in many cases are also auditory experiences, and assures himself of their presence. Thus a new period of experience arises and opens up a new space which we can experience but which nonetheless does not reveal

spektrum, das als Gedächtnisapparat und zugleich als Prophezeiung funktioniert. Über ein bestimmtes Vorwissen können wir das Hör-Äquivalent dieser Bilder abtasten, während unser Auge den Schauwert von Form und Material genießt. Vermeules Bilder verorten sich auf einer nach oben offenen Mobilitätsskala, die einen Rhythmus des Wartens vorgibt, den man, je nach Tagesform, träge, in gestauter Gewohnheit, oder vielleicht doch als musikalischen Impuls empfangen kann.

1)

Andrea Köhler, Lange Weile. Über das Warten, Insel Verlag, Frankfurt am Main und Leipzig, 2007, S. 101

(2)

Johannes Vermeer (Jan Vermeer van Delft) (1632-1675): *Brieflesendes Mädchen am offenen Fenster*, um 1659, Öl auf Leinwand, 83 x 64,5 cm, Gemäldegalerie Alte Meister, Dresden

(3)

Diedrich Diederichsen, 1.500 Schallplatten 1979-1989, Kiepenheuer & Witsch, Köln, 1989, S. 87/88, Ergänzung (17)

(4)

The Specials / *Doesn't make it allright* (1979)

Just because you're nobody. It doesn't mean that you're no good. Just because there's a reason. It doesn't mean it's understood.

It doesn't make it alright. It doesn't make it alright. It's the worst excuse in the world. And it, it doesn't make it alright. Some people think they're really clever. To smash your head against the wall. Then they say „you got it my way". They really think they know it all.

It doesn't make it alright. It doesn't make it alright. It's the worst excuse in the world. And it, it doesn't make it alright. Just because you're a black boy. Just because you're a white. It doesn't mean you've got to hate him. It doesn't mean you've got to fight. It doesn't make it alright. It doesn't make it alright. It's the worst excuse in the world. And it, it doesn't make it alright. Just because you're nobody!

(5)

The Clash / *Police and Thieves* (1977)

Police and thieves in the streets. Oh yeah! Scaring the nation with their guns and ammunition. Police and thieves in the street. Oh yeah! Fighting the nation with their guns and ammunition.From Genesis to Revelation. The next generation will be, hear me. From Genesis to Revelation. The next generation will be, hear me.

And all the crowd walking in day by day. No one stop it in anyway. And all the peace maker turn war officer. Hear what I say. Police, police, police and thieves, oh yeah. Police, police, police and thieves, oh yeah.

From Genesis, oh yeah. Police, police, police and thieves, oh yeah.

And I'm scaring, I'm fighting the nation, oh yeah.

Shooting, shooting their guns and, guns and ammunation, oh yeah. Oh yeah.

...

(6)

„The scene is down to earth, but the feeling is high above ground.", Koen Vermeule in einer E-mail an den Autor vom 03.01.2012

(7)

Den Titel *Morning a Cruel Turmoiler* is hat Koen Vermeule einem irischen Volkslied entnommen, das zu denjenigen zählt, für die Ludwig van Beethoven im Auftrag des schottischen Verlegers George Thomson zwischen 1809 und 1812 Arrangements für ein bis zwei Singstimmen, Violine, Violoncello und Klavier geschrieben hat. In der deutschen Übersetzung des Texts von Alan Boswell taucht folgende Zeile auf, die den Inhalt des Bildes von Vermeule soufflíert: „Der grausame Morgen bringt alles in Aufruhr. Verbannt Behagen und Ruhe ..."

(8)

Joy Division / *Atmosphere* (1980)

Walk in silence, Don't walk away, in silence. See the danger, Always danger, Endless talking, Life rebuilding, Don't walk away. Walk in silence, Don't turn away, in silence. Your confusion, My illusion, Worn like a mask of self-hate, Confronts and then dies. Don't walk away. People like you find it easy, Naked to see, Walking on air. Hunting by the rivers, Through the streets, Every corner abandoned too soon, Set down with due care. Don't walk away in silence, Don't walk away.

its secrets in full. His pictures possess a scattering range that functions both as a means of remembering and as a prophecy. Through a certain previous knowledge we can sense the auditory equivalent of these pictures while our eye enjoys the visual appeal of form and material. Vermeule's pictures are located on a scale of mobility that is has no upward limits. They define a rhythm of waiting that, depending on our form on the day, we can receive sluggishly, in congested habit, or perhaps as a musical impulse.

(1)

Andrea Köhler, Lange Weile . Über das Warten, Insel Verlag, Frankfurt am Main und Leipzig, 2007, p. 101

(2)

Johannes Vermeer (1632-1675): Girl Reading a Letter by an Open Window, ca. 1659, oil on canvas, 83 x 64.5 cm, Gemäldegalerie Alte Meister, Dresden

(3)

Diedrich Diederichsen, 1.500 Schallplatten 1979-1989, Kiepenheuer & Witsch, Cologne, 1989, pp. 87/88, appendix (17)

(4)

The Specials / *Doesn't make it allright* (1979)

Just because you're nobody. It doesn't mean that you're no good. Just because there's a reason. It doesn't mean it's understood. It doesn't make it alright. It doesn't make it alright. It's the worst excuse in the world. And it, it doesn't make it alright. Some people think they're really clever. To smash your head against the wall. Then they say "you got it my way" They really think they know it all.

It doesn't make it alright. It doesn't make it alright. It's the worst excuse in the world. And it, it doesn't make it alright. Just because you're a black boy. Just because you're a white. It doesn't mean you've got to hate him. It doesn't mean you've got to fight. It doesn't make it alright. It doesn't make it alright. It's the worst excuse in the world. And it, it doesn't make it alright. Just because you're nobody!

(5)

The Clash / *Police And Thieves* (1977)

Police and thieves in the streets. Oh yeah! Scaring the nation with their guns and ammunition. Police and thieves in the street. Oh yeah! Fighting the nation with their guns and ammunition.From Genesis to Revelation. The next generation will be, hear me. From Genesis to Revelation. The next generation will be, hear me.

And all the crowd walking in day by day. No one stop it in anyway. And all the peace makers turn war officers. Hear what I say. Police, police, police and thieves, oh yeah. Police, police, police and thieves, oh yeah.

From Genesis, oh yeah. Police, police, police and thieves, oh yeah.And I'm scaring, I'm fighting the nation, oh yeah.

Shooting, shooting their guns and, guns and ammunition, oh yeah. Oh yeah....

(6)

"The scene is down to earth, but the feeling is high above ground." Koen Vermeule in an e-mail to the author dated 03.01.2012

(7)

Koen Vermeule borrowed the title *"Morning a Cruel Turmoiler is"* from an Irish folk song. It is one of those for which Ludwig van Beethoven was commissioned by the Scottish publisher George Thomson to compose arrangements for one or two voices, violin, violoncello and piano between 1809 and 1812. In the German translation of the text by Alan Boswell the following line occurs, which whispers the content of Vermeule's picture: "Der grausame Morgen bringt alles in Aufruhr. Verbannt Behagen und Ruhe ..." ("Morning a Cruel Turmoiler is, Banishes ease and repose")

(8)

Joy Division / *Atmosphere* (1980)

Walk in silence, Don't walk away, in silence. See the danger, Always danger, Endless talking, Life rebuilding, Don't walk away. Walk in silence, Don't turn away, in silence. Your confusion, My illusion, Worn like a mask of self-hate, Confronts and then dies. Don't walk away. People like you find it easy, Naked to see, Walking on air. Hunting by the rivers, Through the streets, Every corner abandoned too soon, Set down with due care. Don't walk away in silence.

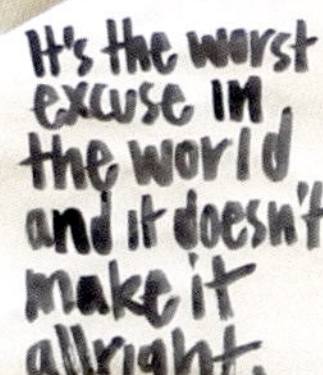
It's the worst
excuse in
the world
and it doesn't
make it
allright.

Police and
thieves
in the street

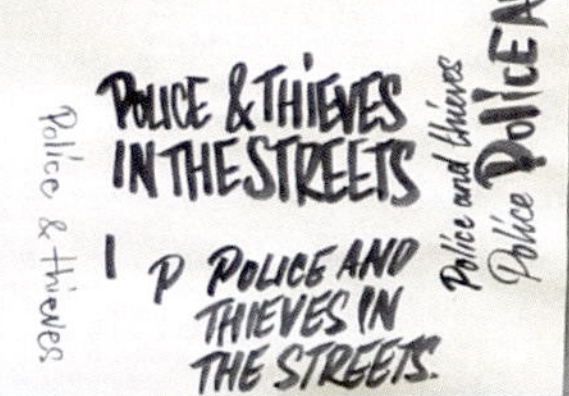
Police & Thieves
in the streets
Police & thieves
P Police and
thieves in
the streets.
Police and thieves

Ghosts, 2008/09
200*300 cm, Öl und Acryl auf Leinwand

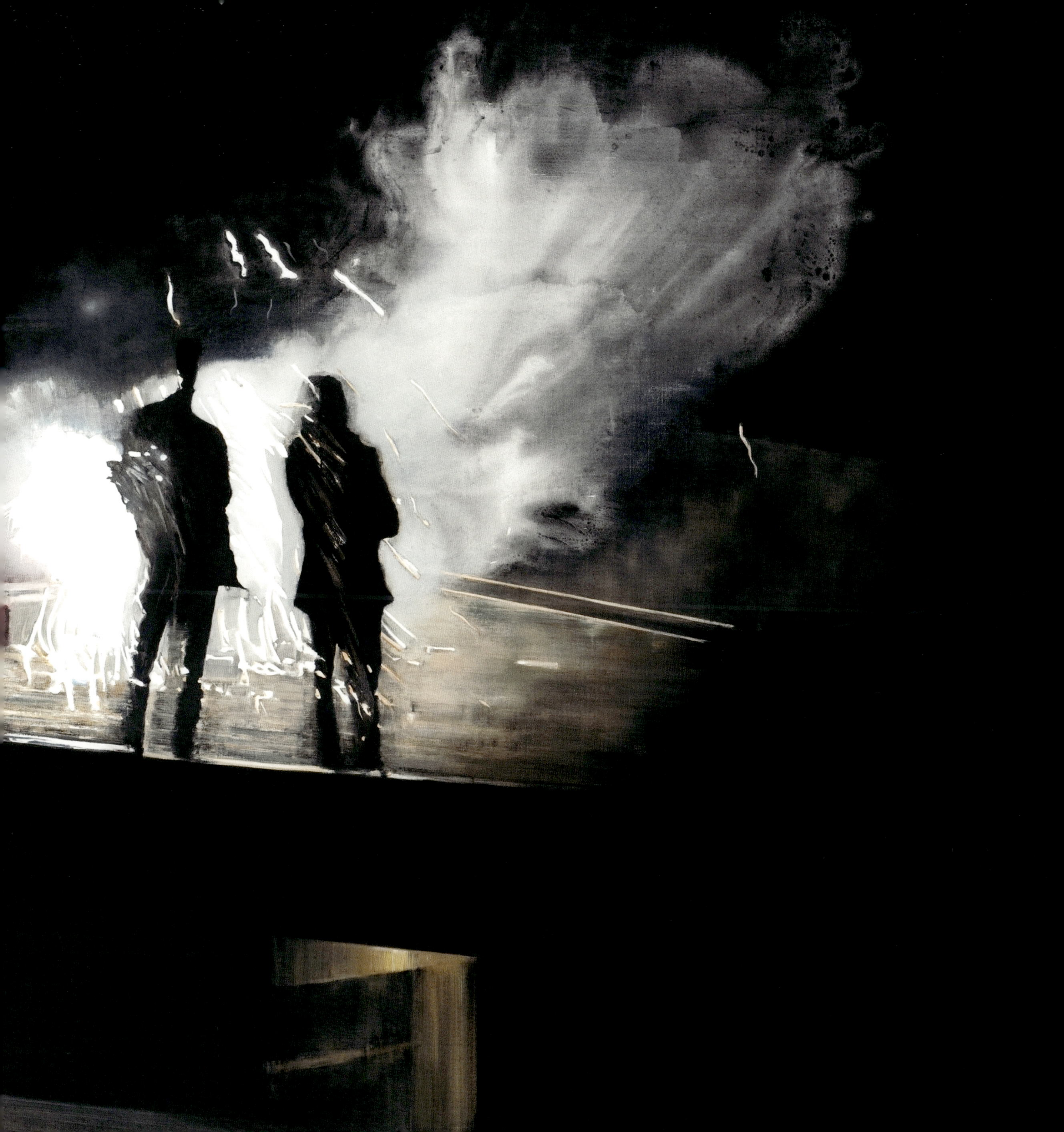

Island, 2011
105*145 cm, Öl und Acryl auf Leinwand

Reading Girl, 2011
150*200 cm, Öl und Acryl auf Leinwand

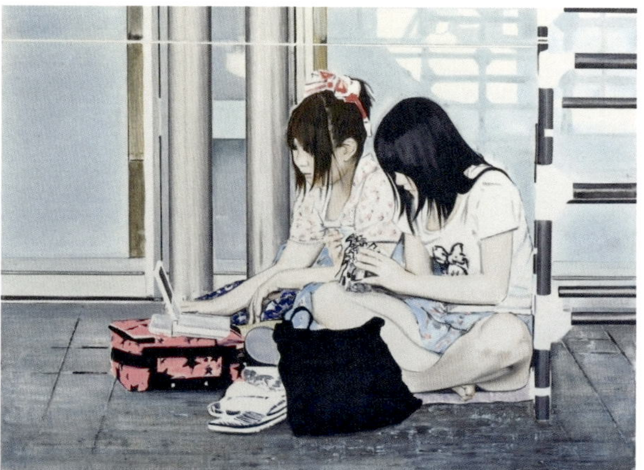

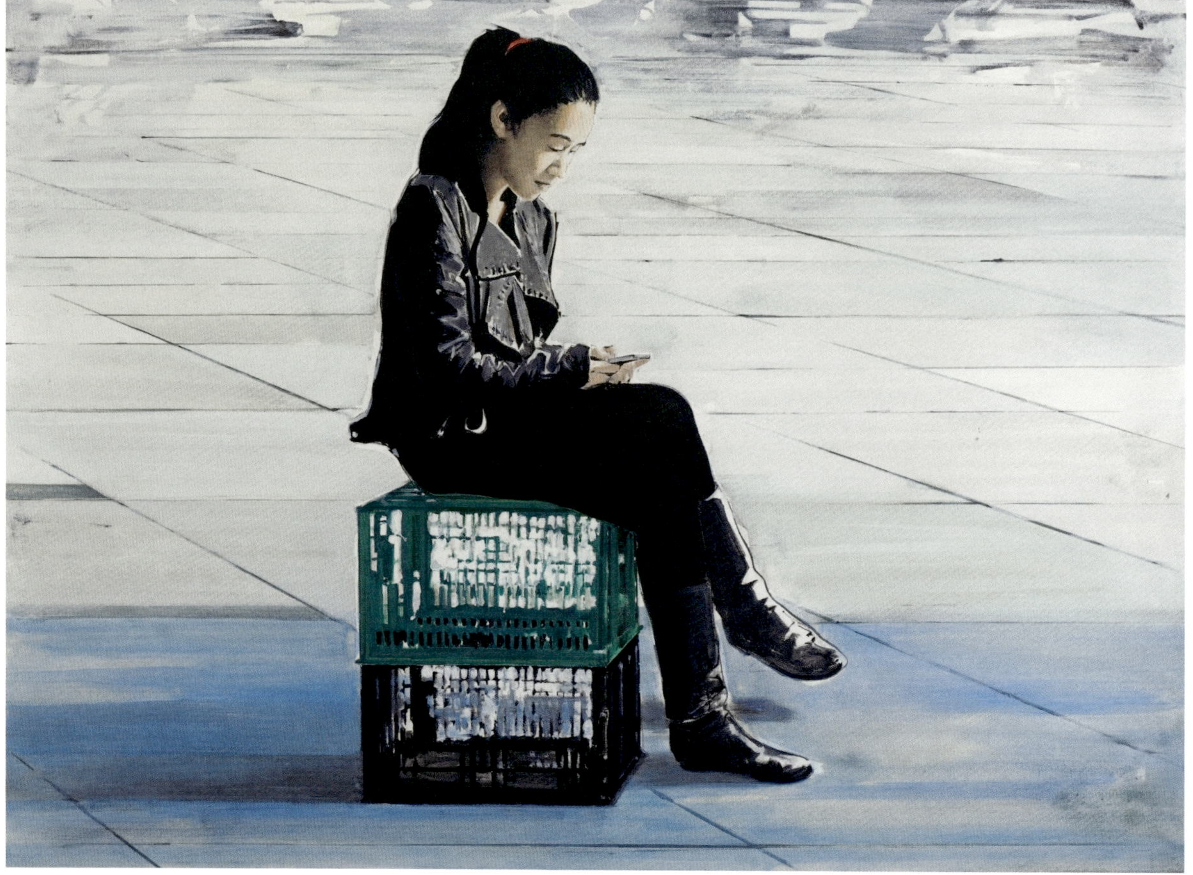

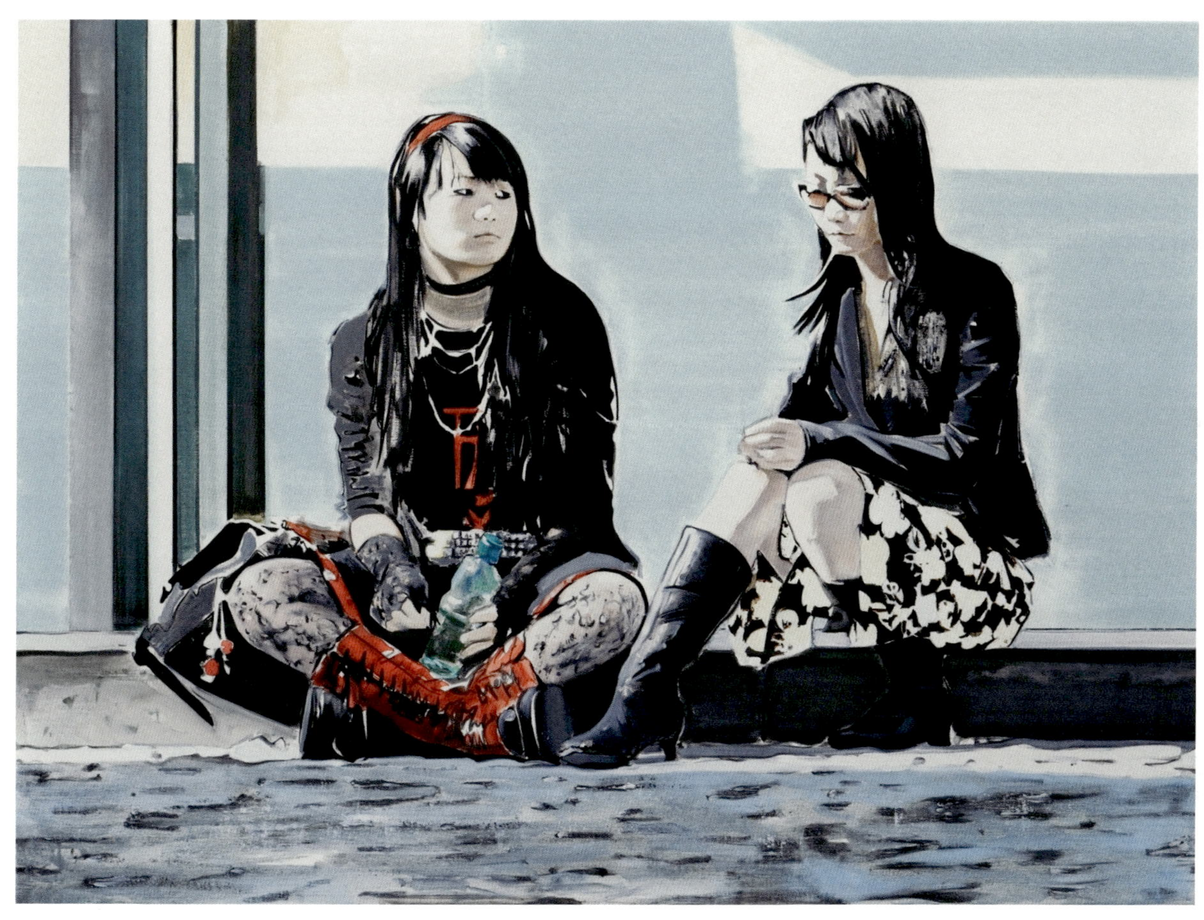

Bored, 2011
105*145 cm, Öl und Acryl auf Leinwand

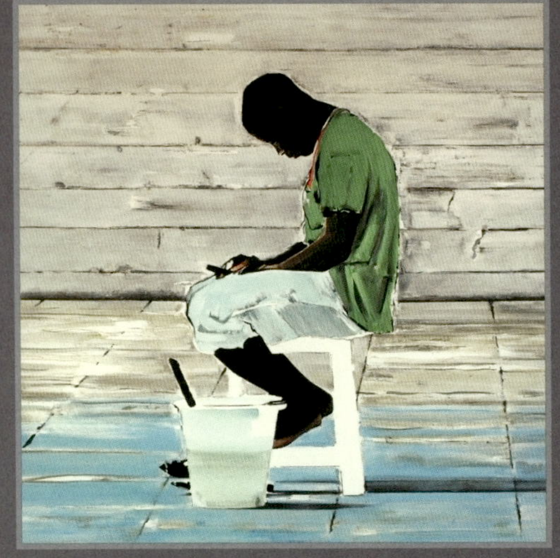
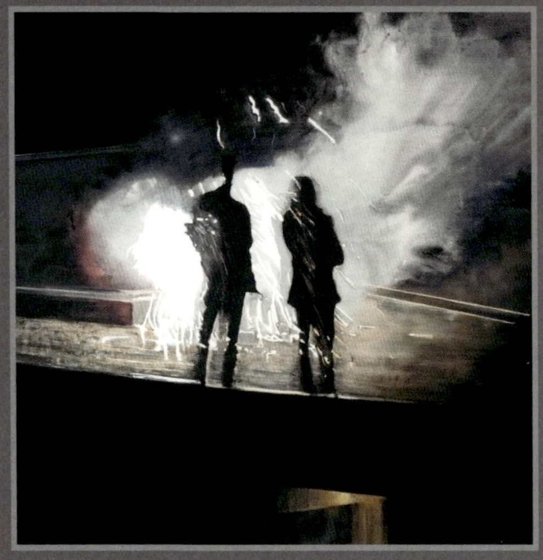
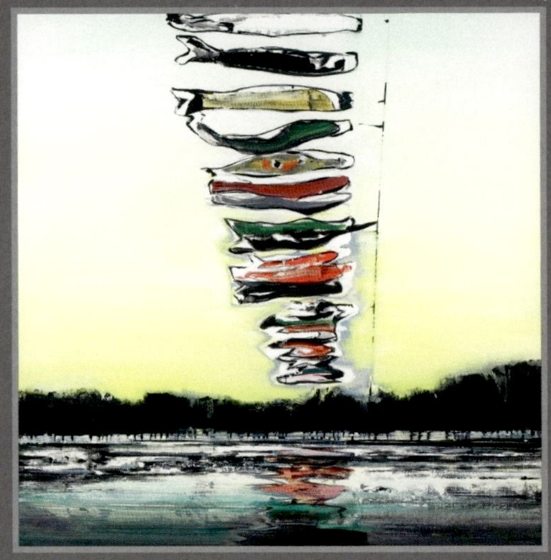
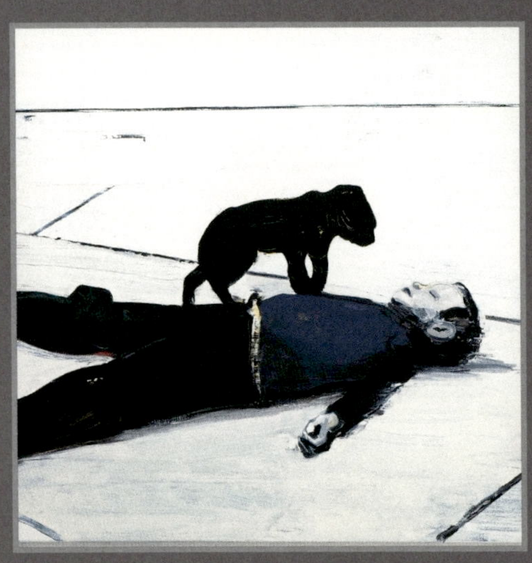
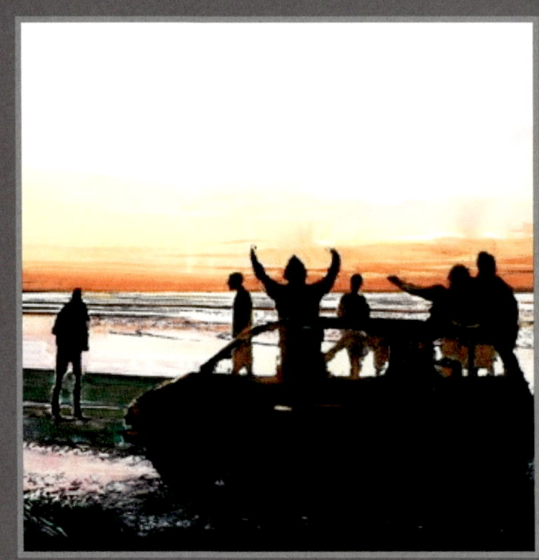
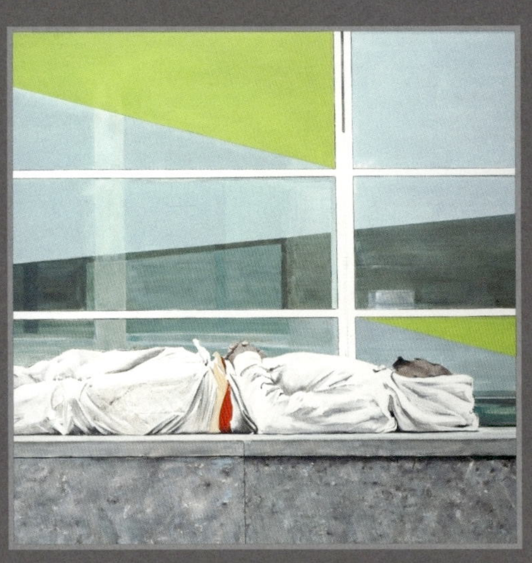
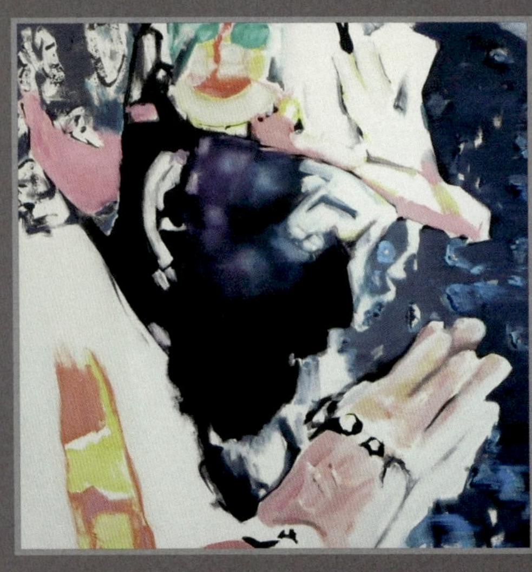
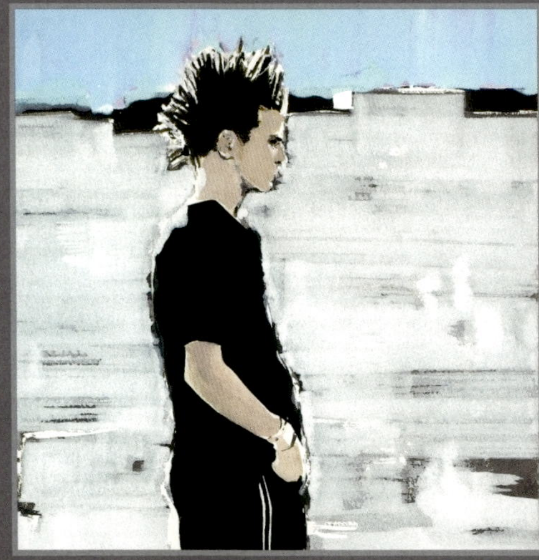
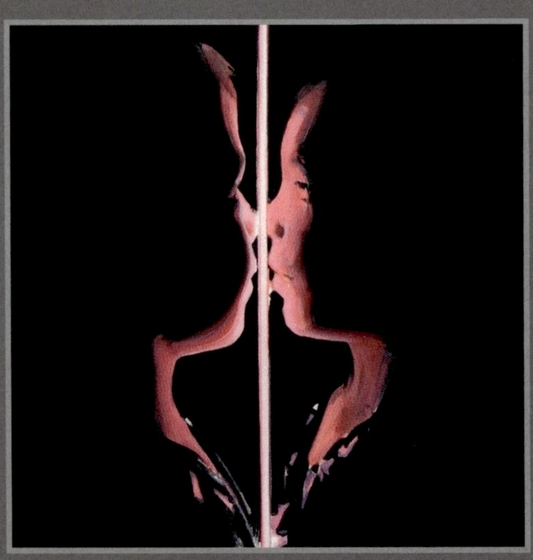

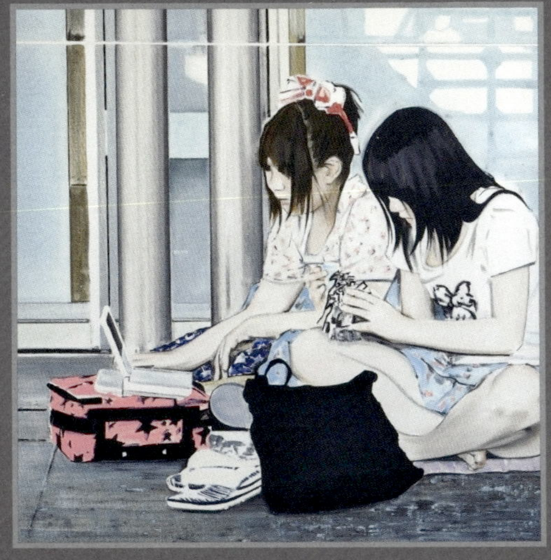
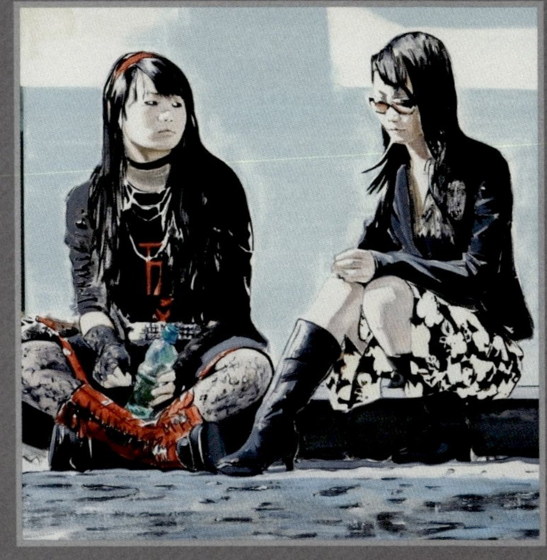
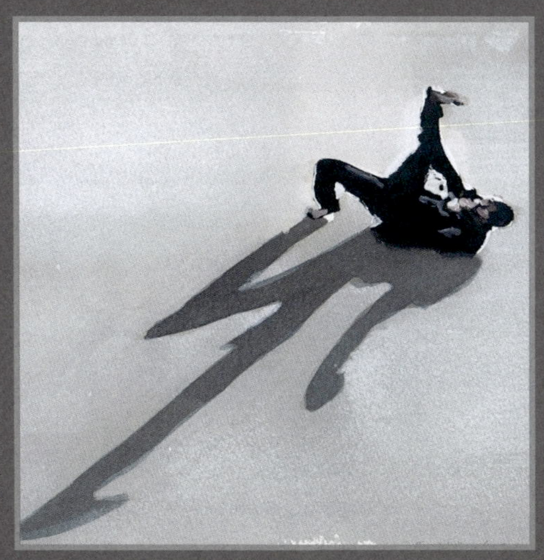
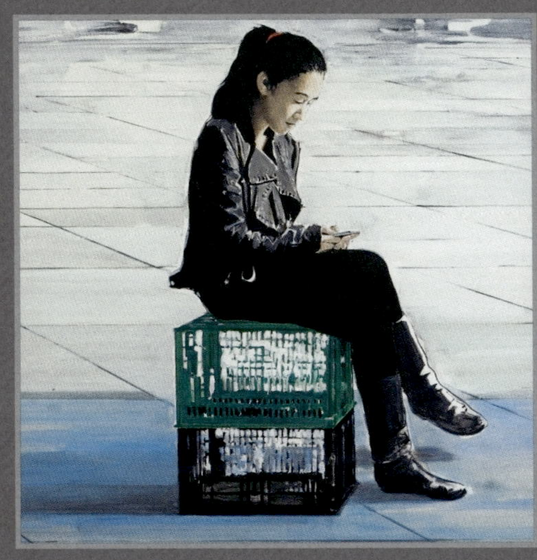
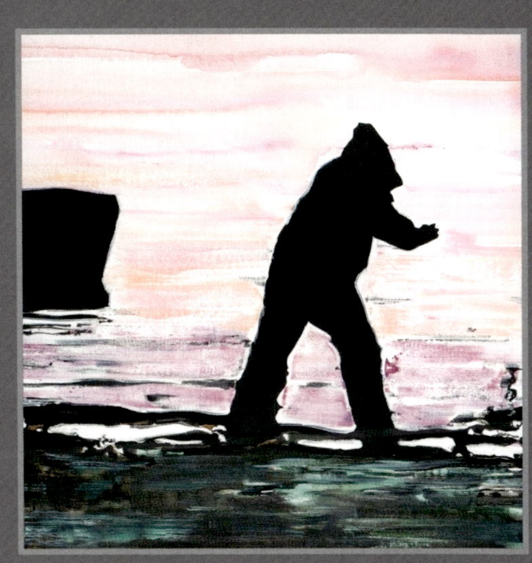
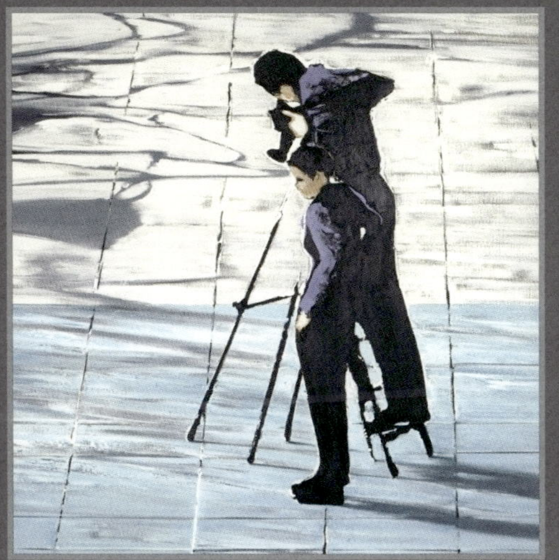
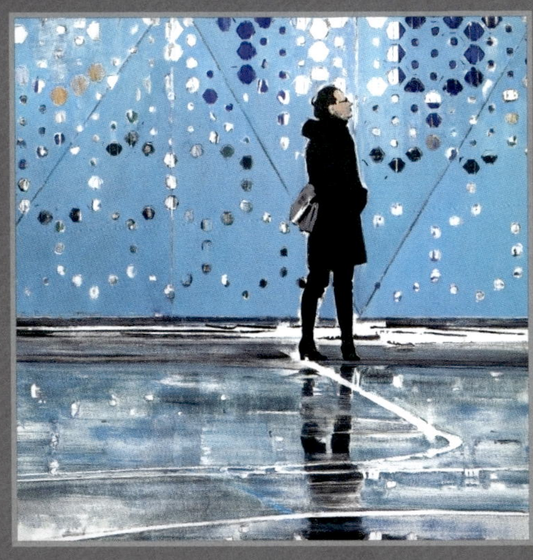
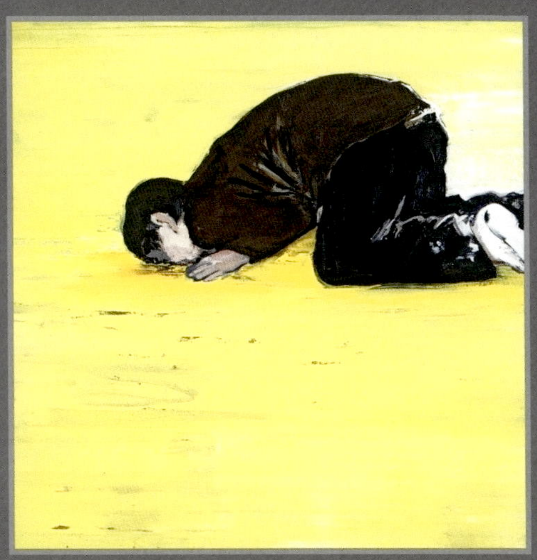
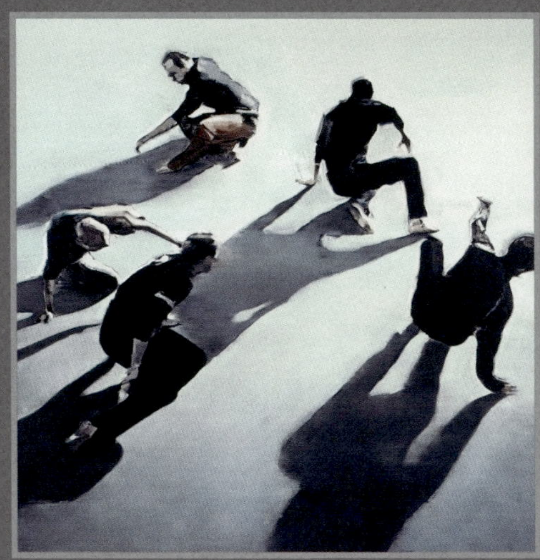

New York Girl 2, 2007
145*105 cm, Öl und Acryl auf Leinwand

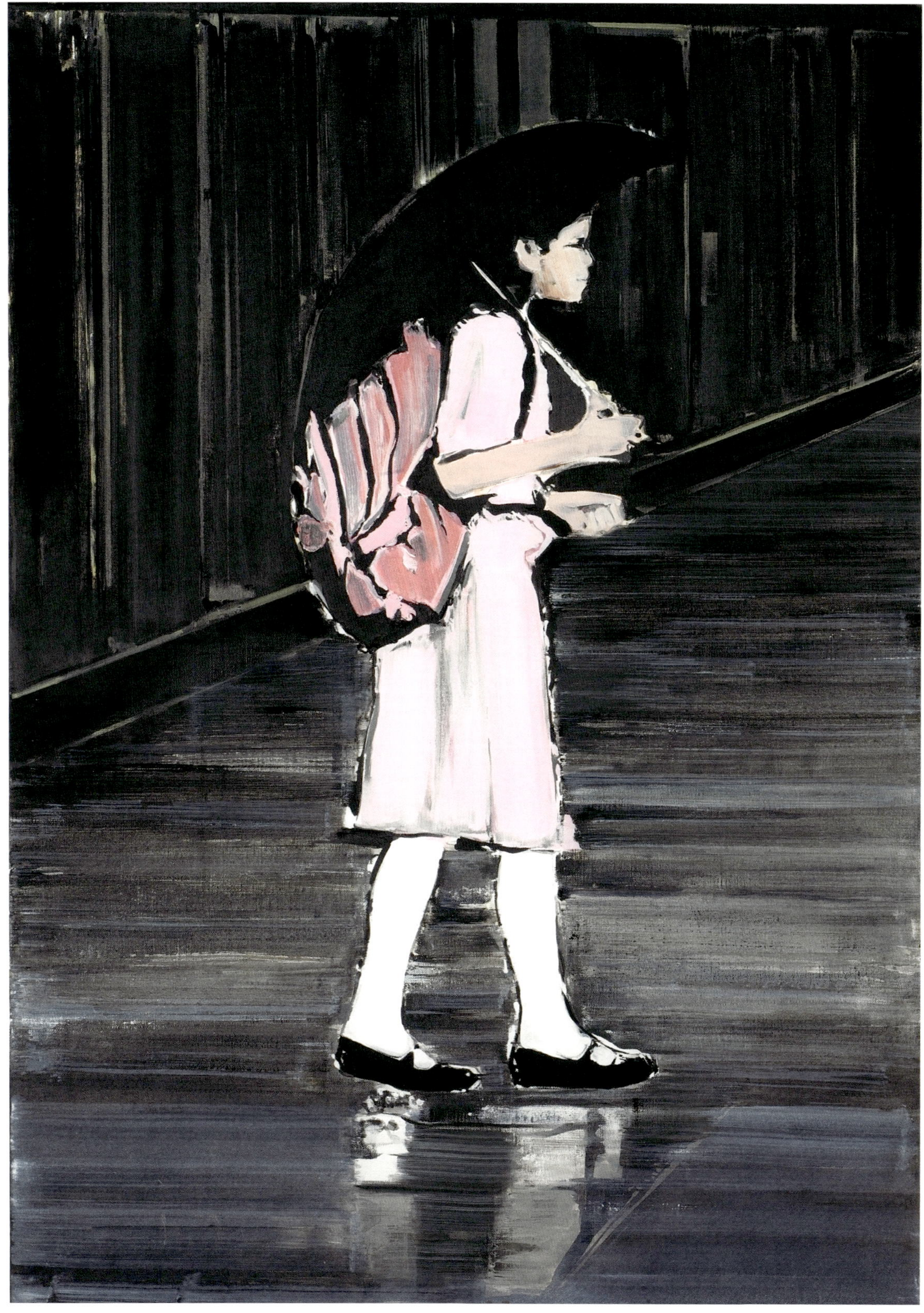

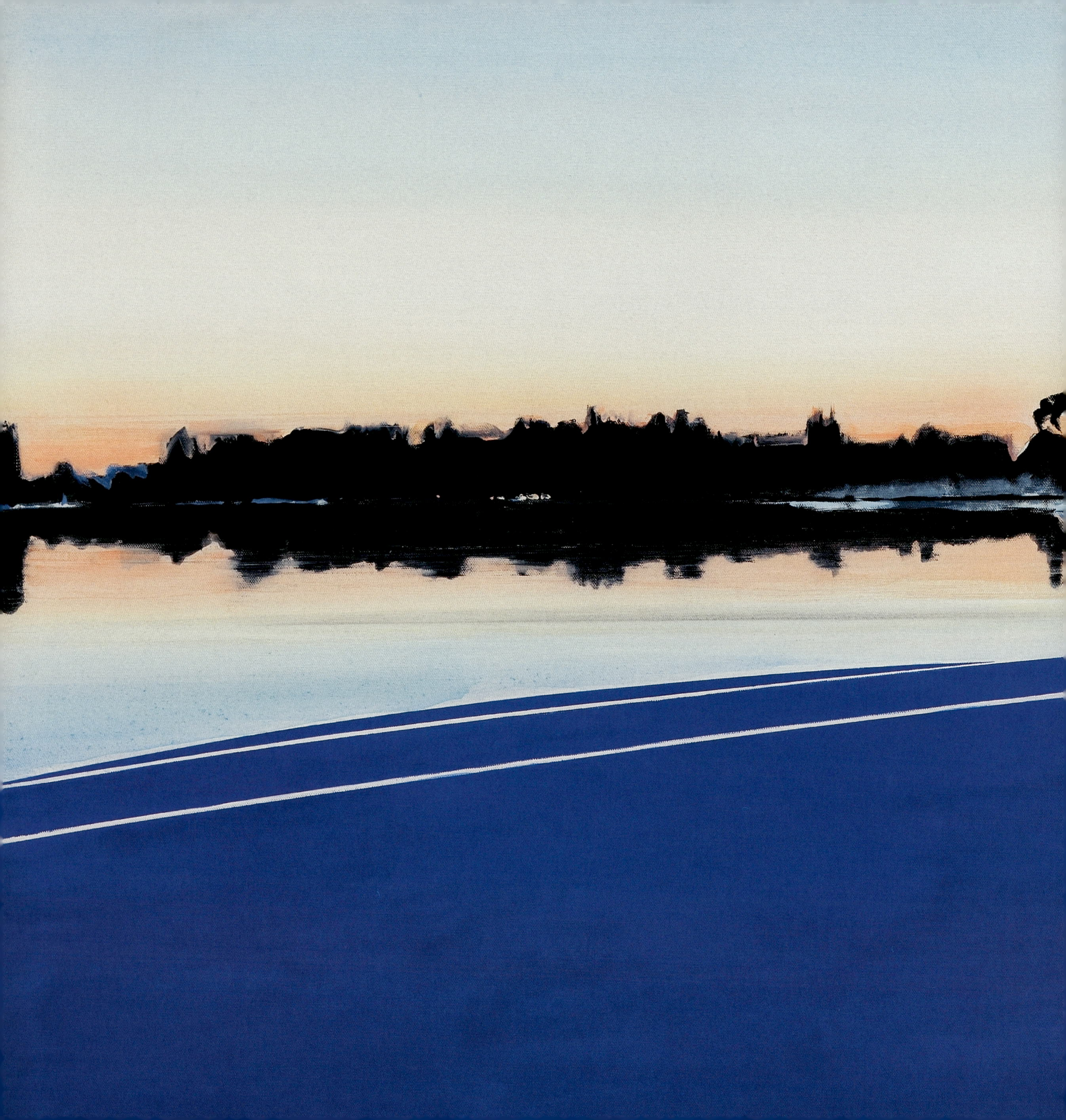

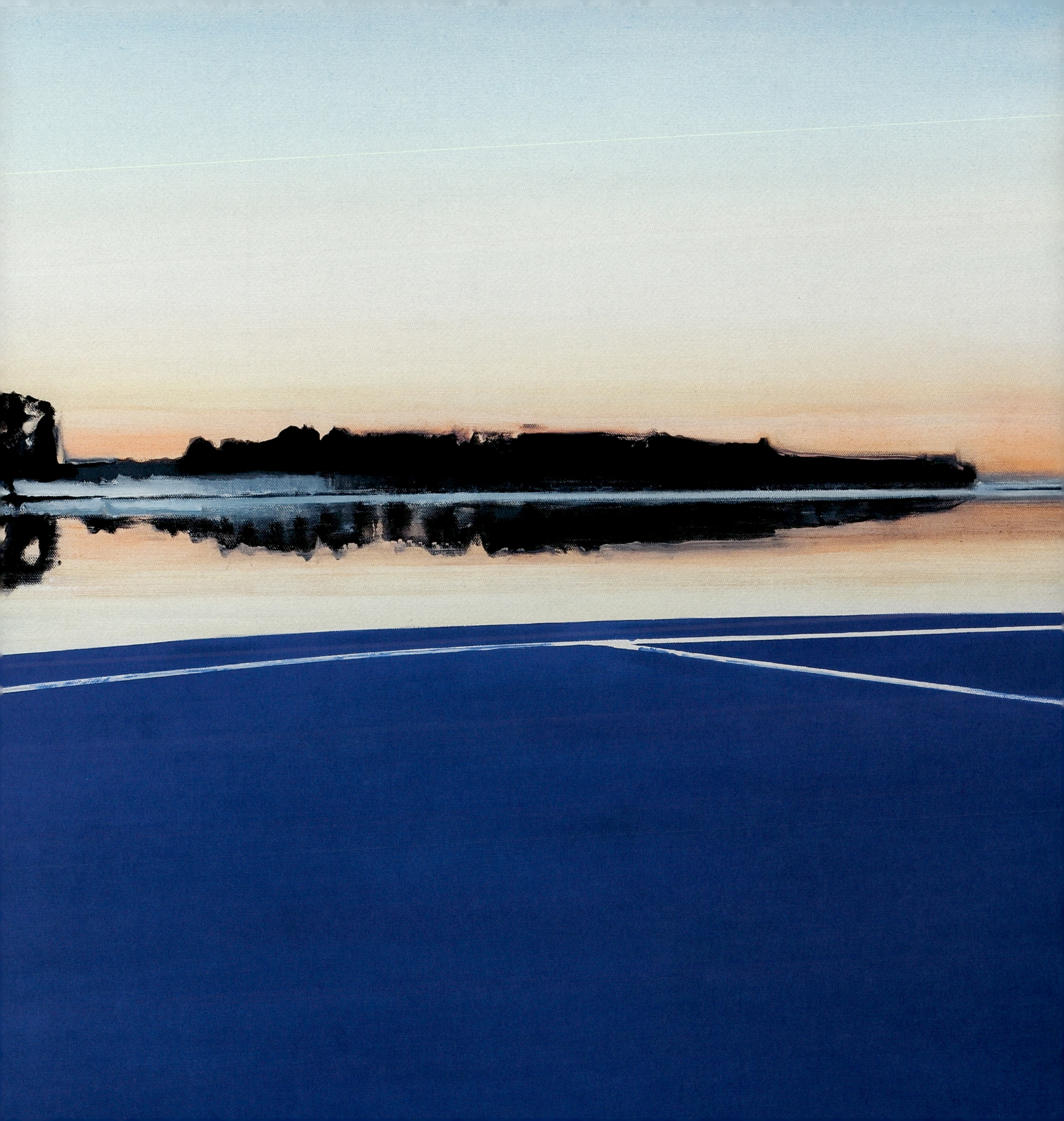

Sunset Blue, 2011
100*200 cm, Öl und Acryl auf Leinwand

Ohne Titel, 1993
170*340 cm, Öl und Acryl auf Leinwand

Morning a Cruel Turmoiler is, 2007
105*145 cm, Öl und Acryl auf Leinwand

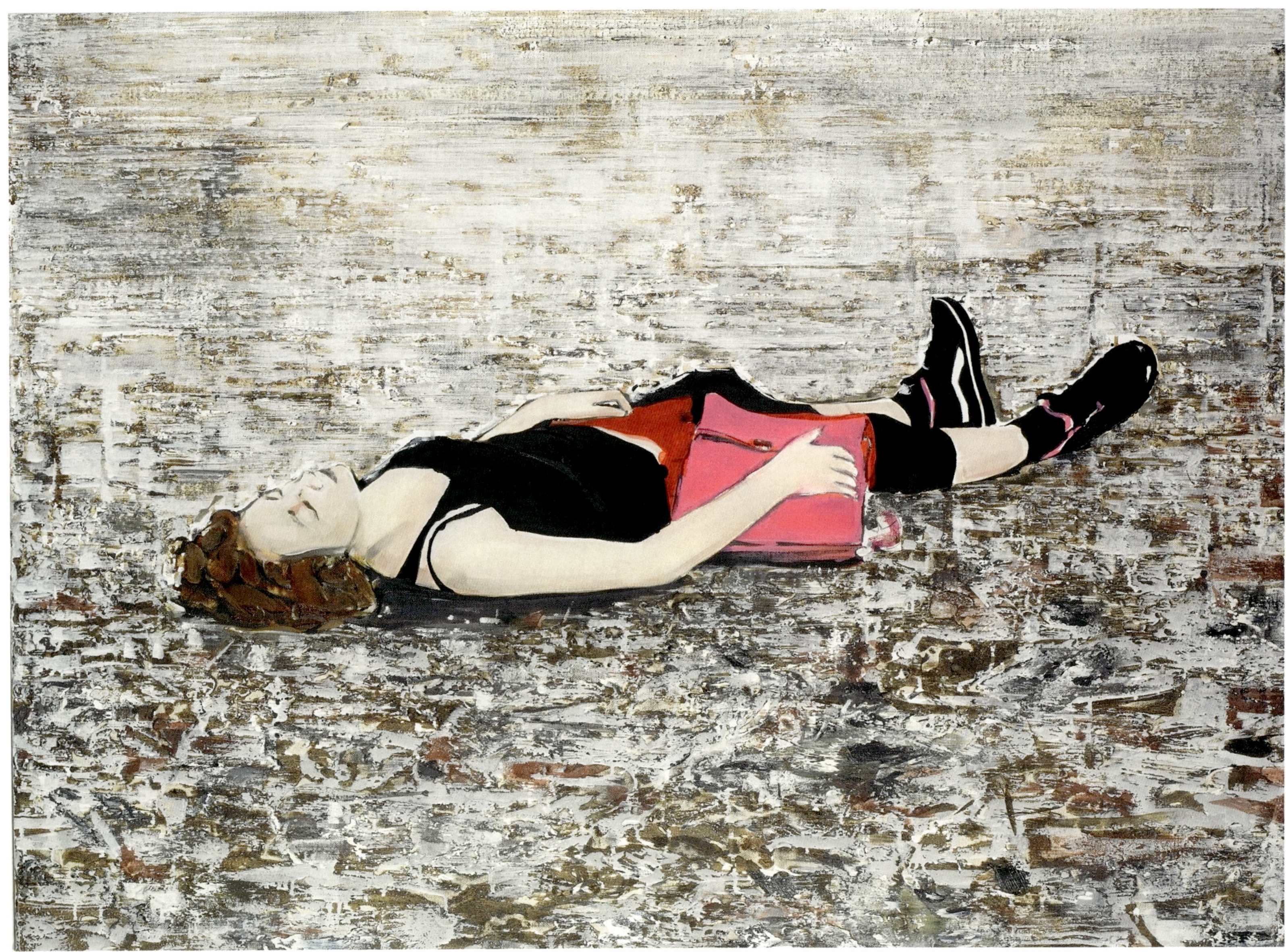

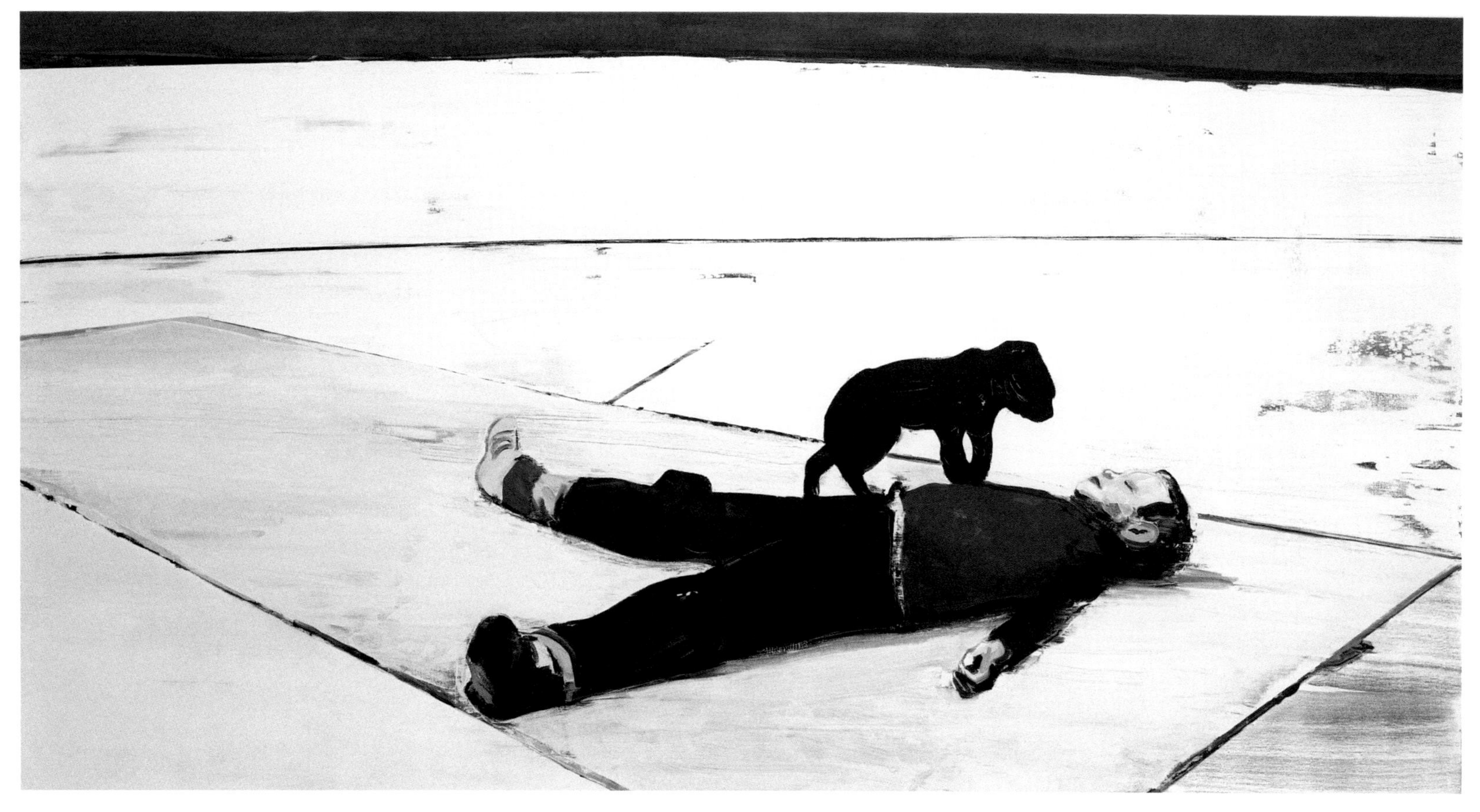

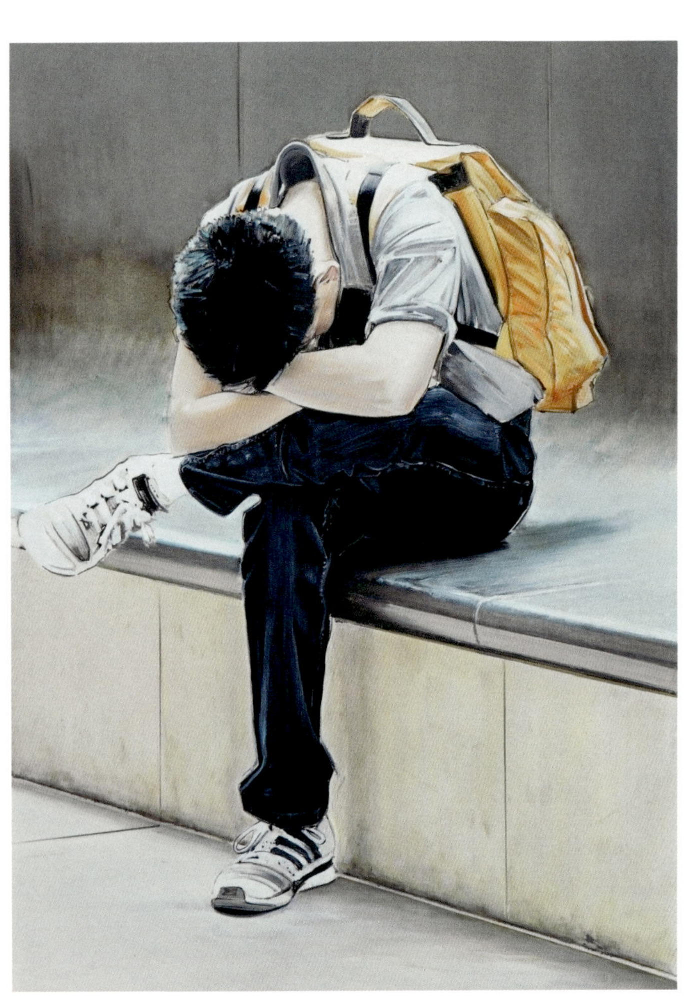

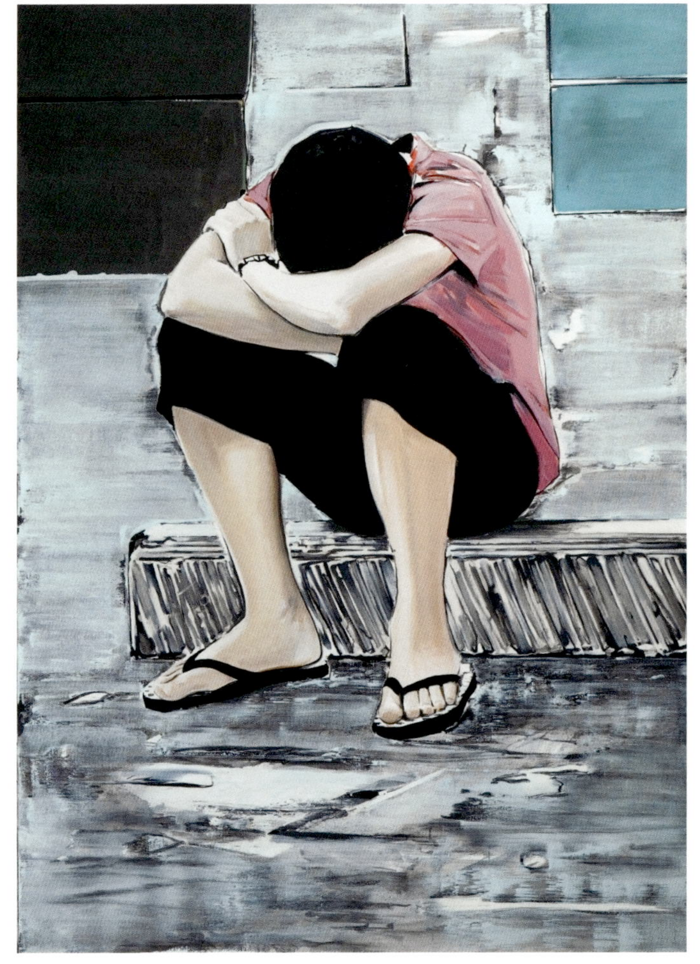

Le Dormeur, 2011
200*145 cm, Öl und Acryl auf Leinwand

Dreamer, 2011
200*145 cm, Öl und Acryl auf Leinwand

Eine unvollendete Reise | An Unfinished Journey

Heike Endter

Vielleicht lag es daran, dass im Museum Brandhorst – gleich schräg gegenüber der Galerie Wittenbrink, in der ich an diesem Text schreibe – die Videoarbeit *Ten Thousand Waves* von Isaac Julien lief, dass mich Koen Vermeulens Bild *5.00 pm* an Formen unsicherer und oft auch unglückseliger Migration per Boot erinnerte. Es wäre leicht gewesen, zum Telefon zu greifen, um in Amsterdam anzurufen und den Maler zu fragen, ob diese Assoziation dem Ursprung seines Bildes gerecht wird. Oder ob es sich vielmehr um die Darstellung von mehreren Fischern handelt, die am Nachmittag in einem kleinen Boot aufbrechen. (es soll so etwas wie Nachtfischen geben.) Die Männer könnten auch gerade im flachen Wasser angekommen sein.

Gewissheit ist gut, nur manchmal unfruchtbar. Der Grund für die spezielle Assoziation darüber, was die Männer mit dem Boot vorhaben könnten, liegt schließlich nicht nur in Juliens Video. Vielmehr hat die Assoziation die gleiche Quelle wie das Video, und das sind die medialen Bilder, mit denen Migration auf dem Seeweg wiedergegeben wird, wie sie sich an südeuropäischen Küsten abspielt.[1]

Daraus lässt sich Verschiedenes für die Bedingtheit des eigenen Sehens (Erkennens) ableiten. Zunächst einmal spielt der eigene europäische Standpunkt eine Rolle, aus dem heraus das Bild wahrgenommen wird. Vermutlich, und sehr wahrscheinlich, deckt sich dieser mit dem Standpunkt des Malers, der, wie erwähnt in Amsterdam lebt, der eine

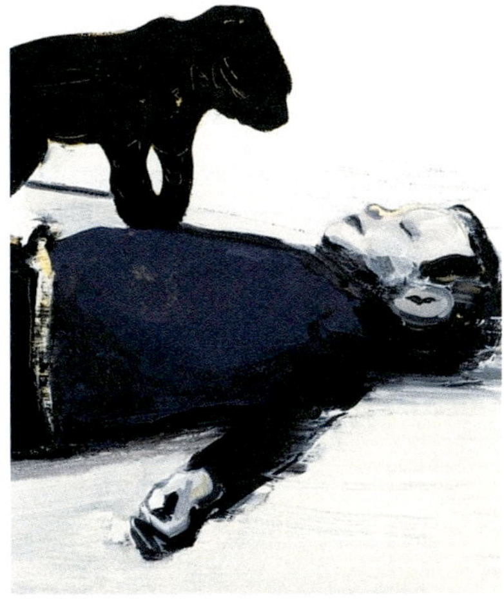

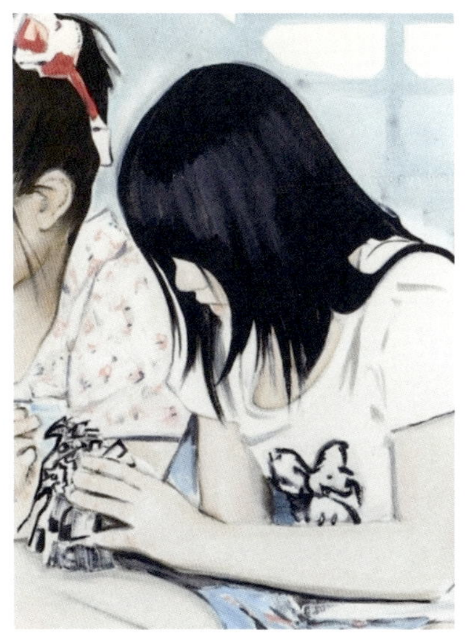

Maybe it was because Isaac Julien's video work *Ten Thousand Waves* was running in the Museum Brandhorst, diagonally across from the Galerie Wittenbrink, where I was working on this text, that Koen Vermeule's picture *5.00 pm* made me think of unsafe and often ill-fated migrations by boat. It would have been easy enough to pick up the telephone and call Amsterdam in order to ask the artist whether this association does justice to the origins of his picture. Or whether he was concerned with portraying a group of fishermen setting off in a small boat in the afternoon. (Fishing at night is apparently something that people do.) Or the men might have just arrived in the shallow water.

Certainty is good, albeit sometimes unproductive. Ultimately, the reason for the special association relating to what the men in the boat might be planning to do does not lie only in Julien's video. In fact, the association has the same source as the video, namely the pictures in the media in which migration by sea is depicted, and how it takes place along the coasts of south-east Europe. [1]

Here we can derive various ideas regarding the relativity of our own seeing (perception). First of all there is our own European point of view which plays a role here, the standpoint from which we perceive the image. Presumably, indeed very probably, this overlaps with that of the artist who, as already mentioned, lives in Amsterdam, and has a white skin and a very Dutch-sounding name, so that we have no reason to suspect a migration story within his family. In addition to his pictures of people he also paints large-format, wonderful landscapes that are so flatly Dutch, so neatly structured and cultivated or characterized by the omnipresent water in that country, that we can find no evidence of exotic connections here either.

The people in the picture *5.00 pm*, young men plus a boy, are dark-skinned. At least physically they clearly do not belong in the usual, European context that is determined by the white majority. But if we try to find a potentially European context for their action, then it is a migration that springs to mind, a journey that will take them away from their homeland and towards Europe.

The place where they have been painted has not been depicted in much detail and thus appears to be a sea-like expanse of water which could really be anywhere. Only if we assume that it corresponds with their original homeland, can we arrive at a possible interpretation in which the men are fishermen. (Although the boy surprises us, because he seems far more interested in swimming than in the arduous task of catching fish. In fact, though, it is not so much the boy who is strange; what is really odd is the number of men compared with the size of their boat.)

weiße Hautfarbe und einen vollkommen niederländisch klingenden Namen hat, so dass man keine Migrationsgeschichte innerhalb seiner Familie vermuten muss. Neben seinen Darstellungen von Menschen malt er großformatige, wundervolle Landschaften, die so niederländisch eben, durchstrukturiert und bewirtschaftet oder von dem in diesem Land allseits präsenten Wasser geprägt sind, dass sich auch hier keine exotischen Zusammenhänge finden lassen.

Die Personen auf dem Bild *5.00 pm* – bei ihnen handelt es sich um junge Männer plus einen Jungen – haben eine dunkle Hautfarbe. Sie gehören offenbar nicht in den gewöhnlichen, von einer weißen Mehrheit bestimmten europäischen Kontext, zumindest nicht durch ihre Körper. Versucht man aber für ihre Handlung einen möglichen europäischen Kontext zu finden, dann ist es der einer Migration, einer Wanderungsbewegung, die sie von zu Hause fort nach Europa führt.

Nur wenn man annimmt, der Ort, an dem sie abgebildet sind – dieser Ort ist nicht besonders detailiert gemalt und darum ein denkbar ortsneutrales meerartiges Gewässer – entspräche ihrer originären Heimat, ergibt sich eine mögliche Interpretation der Männer als Fischer, wobei der Junge verblüfft, der viel mehr am Baden als am mühsamen Einfangen von Fischen interessiert zu sein scheint. Eigentlich ist weniger der Junge seltsam. Es verwundert die Zahl der Männer im Vergleich zur Größe ihres Bootes.

Nun ließe sich einwenden, dieses Rätsel betreffe schließlich nur das eine Bild in Koen Vermeules Werk, weshalb es auch auf sein Werk nicht verallgemeinernd anwendbar sei und deshalb nicht über Gebühr strapaziert werden müsste. Allerdings schließt sich an eben jenes erste Erstaunen, welches das Bild *"5.00 pm"* ausgelöst hat, eine andere Beobachtung an, nämlich die, dass auf mehreren anderen von Vermeulens Bildern asiatisch aussehende Menschen wiedergegeben sind. Auch hierfür gibt es keinen im Bild selbst erkennbaren oder anderweitig offensichtlichen Grund. Die Orte, an denen sich diese Menschen aufhalten sind nicht bezeichnet und kaum lokalisierbar. Die zwei Mädchen des Bildes *Bored* könnten sich an einer Bushaltestelle sowohl in Amsterdam als auch in Japan aufhalten. Den Jungen aus *Tokyo Dreamer* scheint es an einen Flughafen verschlagen zu haben, wo er sich nun, mangels eines eigenen Bettes, zusammenkauert und ausruht. Dieser Flughafen, sollte es einer sein, ist ebenso ortsunspezifisch wie die vermutete Bushaltestelle. Er könnte an fast jedem Ort der Welt liegen, an dem für derartige Bauten viel Glas und glattpolierte Bodenplatten verbaut wurden.

Dieser Fußboden ist übrigens fast wie eine Wasserfläche gemalt. Auffällig ist, dass dieser Künstler mehmals die Böden innerhalb architektonischer Räume so behandelt, als seien sie

We could, of course, object that this riddle only applies to this one picture in Koen Vermeule's oeuvre, which is why it is not applicable to his work in general and should therefore not be over-emphasized unduly. However, the initial amazement that *5.00 pm* aroused sparked off another observation, namely that in several other paintings by Vermeule we can see pictures of Asian-looking people. Here, too, there is no apparent or otherwise obvious in the picture. The places where the people are shown are not named and virtually impossible to localize. The two girls in the picture Bored could be at a bus stop in Amsterdam or in Japan. The boy in *Tokyo Dreamer* appears to have ended up at an airport, where for want of a proper bed of his own he has curled up and is taking a rest. The airport, if indeed that is what it is, is just as unspecific a location as the putative bus stop. It could be virtually anywhere in the world where large areas of glass and polished floor tiles are used in the constructions of buildings of this type.

The floor, incidentally, is painted almost like an expanse of water. It is noticeable that on several occasions Vermeule treats the floors within architectural spaces as if they were water: they sparkle and reflect, are smooth or rough and above all blue, while the ground in his landscapes has a similar structure to paved squares or corridors in buildings. For example, the picture of an open field in Scape is not so far removed from the floor of the airport in *Tokyo Dreamer*, which appears similarly free and open.
The sum of possible locations for this airport is, in any case, virtually unlimited. Depending on where we hypothetically place this unlocatable and yet concrete place, we would have to decide in which direction the boy is potentially intending to move. After all, he is at an airport. Is he waiting and daydreaming of a journey back to his home country? Or does he wish to get away from there? In this respect, the title *Tokyo Dreamer* tells us very little.

The attempts at concrete (national) localization are thus fruitless but not unimportant. Because if the artist's attention is focused on a hitherto unfounded exoticism (foreignness, exception, distance), it also refers to an urbaneness (a cosmopolitan existence). The artist himself can appear as a traveler who paints what he sees during his journey. But he can equally find himself in a static position, from which he adopts the permanent traveling of other people into his pictures.

And now, at the latest, three other pictures and their titles acquire a certain importance. I am referring to the pictures *Glasshouse*, *Island* and *Le Départ*, and judging by the titles all three allow us to conclude a somewhat uncertain relationship to a homeland, wherever that may be. Upon seeing the word "glasshouse" we may find ourselves thinking of the well-known recommendation: "People who live in glasshouses shouldn't throw stones." The man in the picture most definitely does not seem inclined to such activity at the moment. He is lying

aus Wasser: Sie glitzern und spiegeln, sind glatt oder gekräuselt und vor allem blau. Während die Böden in seinen Landschaften ähnlich strukturiert sind wie mit Platten belegte Plätze oder Gebäudeflure. Zum Beispiel ist das Bild eines offenen Feldes in *Scape* gar nicht so weit entfernt vom ähnlich frei und offen wirkenden Boden des Flughafens in *Tokyo Dreamer*.

Die Summe möglicher Standorte dieses Flughafens ist jedenfalls kaum überschaubar. Je nachdem, wohin man diesen unlokalisierbaren und dennoch konkreten Ort hypothetisch verlegt, müsste man entscheiden, wohin sich die potentielle Fortbewegung des Jungen richtet. Schließlich ist er an einem Flughafen. Wartet er träumend auf eine Reise zurück nach Hause? Oder wünscht er sich gerade, von dort fortzukommen? Der Titel *Tokyo Dreamer* verrät in dieser Hinsicht nicht viel.

Insofern sind die Versuche konkreter (nationaler) Lokalisierungen zwar unergiebig aber nicht unwichtig. Denn wenn das Augenmerk des Künstlers auf einer – bis hierher – unbegründeten Exotik (Exotik: Fremdheit, Ausnahme, Ferne) liegt, verweist es auch auf eine Weltgewandtheit (ein kosmopolitisches Dasein). Der Künstler selbst kann als Reisender auftreten, der malt, was er unterwegs beobachtet. Aber genauso gut kann er sich in einem statischen Zustand befinden, von dem aus er die permanenten Reisetätigkeiten anderer Menschen in seine Bilder aufnimmt.

Spätestens jetzt fallen drei weitere Bilder und deren Titel ins Gewicht. Es sind die Bilder *Glasshouse*, *Island* und *Le Depar*t und dem Titel nach lassen alle drei auf eine etwas ungewisse Beziehung zu einer wo auch immer verorteten Heimat schließen. Bei dem Wort "glasshouse" kann man an die bekannte Empfehlung denken: Wer im Glashaus sitzt, soll nicht mit Steinen werfen. Definitiv neigt der Mann im Bild momentan nicht zu einer solchen Aktivität. Er liegt und ruht. Der Spruch ist übrigens nicht aus der Bibel, auch wenn er klingt, als ob er diesem Buch entstammen könnte. Denkt man darüber nach, passt die Zeit der Bibelnotation auch nicht zum erstmaligen Aufkommen gläserner Häuser (die deutschen Entsprechungen für "glasshouse" sind neben Gewächshaus auch Atelier und Flugzeugkanzel). Interessanterweise vergleicht Cornel Bierens den Mann von "Glasshouse" mit Christus, so wie er in Hans Holbeins *Der tote Christus im Grab* entsetzlich eingezwängt, fast nackt und mager, mit offen stehenden Augen und Mund, und beunruhigend verfärbter Haut daliegt.[2] Nun ist der Liegende bei Koen Vermeule in den genannten Details das Gegenteil davon. Er hat zudem die Beine übereinander geschlagen, was einen entspannten Eindruck hervorruft und eine Körperhaltung ist, die von Bestattern eher nicht als die letztlich bleibende angestrebt wird. Das heißt, glücklicherweise ist nicht jeder, liegt er erst einmal, auch tot. Aber diese Unschärfe ist durchaus vertraut (kennen Sie die Sage, dass Elefanten, wenn sie sich hinlegen, bald sterben?). Auffällig ist vor allem der Platz, an dem sich der Mann ausgestreckt hat. Denn seiner intimen, ruhenden Haltung zum Trotz, wirkt der Ort, den er dafür gewählt hat, wie ein

and resting. The saying, incidentally, does not come from the Bible, although it sounds as if it might do. On reflection, it becomes clear that the time when the Bible was written does not coincide with the first appearance of houses made of glass. (The German equivalents of "glasshouse" are not only a greenhouse but also a studio and an aircraft cockpit.) Interestingly enough, Cornel Bierens compares the man in *Glasshouse* with Christ, as he lies there in Hans Holbein's *The Body of the Dead Christ in the Tomb*, horribly wedged in, thin and almost naked, with staring eyes and open mouth and disturbingly discoloured skin. [2] The man lying there in Koen Vermeule's picture displays the very opposite of these characteristics. Moreover, he has crossed his legs over each other, which gives an impression of relaxation and is a posture that undertakers would be reluctant to recreate as the last, the final one. That means that fortunately not everyone who is lying down like that is actually dead. But this vagueness is certainly familiar. (Have you heard of the myth that when elephants lie down they are about to die?) What is remarkable is above all the place where the man has stretched out. Because in spite of his intimate, relaxed posture, the place he has chosen for it looks as if it is a public one. Not only the large glass façade, but also the long, stone ledge in front of it, hardly look as if they belong to a private house. Of course, even that could be possible, because one of the features of modern architecture involves the blurring of the mutually exclusive relationship between inside and outside through the use of glass surfaces – whereby this also changes the relationship between private and public.

But irrespective of whether the reclining man is currently in his house, a personal form of homeland, or in a building which is accessible to the public, he has certainly chosen a transparent, bright and potentially vulnerable enclosure. Here, in complete serenity, he claims a resting place for himself, which his to say: he occupies it and makes it his own. This behavior is respectfully accepted by the artist and by the perspective he relays to the public.

The motive of the elementary ability to be able to define a place anywhere and at any time as home can be found not only in *Glasshouse*, but also in *Tokyo Dreamer* and *Island*. In each case it is a matter of the temporary occupation of a public space, which is thereby rededicated as a private one. The fact that these actually are temporary occupations is not unimportant. Because what would happen if the impression arose that the people in the pictures had permanently relocated their home to these public streets and locations? The contemporary nomads, who pause during this state of being on the move in a public environment and define the short stages of their journey, would become homeless people. Their ability to establish a sort of home anywhere at all would point to the loss of their original home. While in the pictures of Koen Vermeule we need assume only a temporary absence from these familiar and protected places. In the pictures mentioned, therefore, he records a distinctive and universally observed feature of contemporary societies. What is shown

öffentlicher. Nicht nur die große Glasfront, auch der lange, steinerne Sims davor, scheinen nicht unbedingt einem privaten Haus zugehörig. Natürlich wäre auch das denkbar. Denn es gehört zu den Gesten moderner Architektur durch Glasflächen das einander ausschließende Verhältnis von innen und außen zu verwischen. Womit auch das Verhältnis von privatem und öffentlichem Lebensgefühl verändert wird.

Aber ganz gleich, ob sich der liegende Mann in seinem Haus, einer persönlichen Form der Heimat also, aufhält oder in einem öffentlich zugänglichen Gebäude, so hat er sich doch ein durchscheinendes, helles und für Beschädigungen durchaus anfälliges Gehäuse auserkoren. Hier beansprucht er in größter Gelassenheit einen Ruheort, was heißt, dass er ihn okkupiert und zu seinem eigenen macht. Dieses Verhalten wird durch den Maler und durch seine an das Publikum weitergegebene Perspektive respektvoll akzeptiert.

Das Motiv jener elementaren Fähigkeit, jederzeit und überall ein Heim definieren zu können, findet sich sowohl in *Glasshouse*, als auch in *Tokyo Dreamer* und *Island*. Dabei handelt es sich jeweils um temporäre Okkupationen eines öffentlichen Raums, der somit in einen privaten umgewidmet wird. Dass es sich tatsächlich um temporäre Besetzungen handelt ist nicht unwichtig. Denn was würde geschehen, entstünde der Eindruck, dass die Dargestellten ihr Heim dauerhaft auf öffentliche Straßen und Plätze verlegt hätten? Aus den zeitgenössischen Nomaden, die in öffentlicher Umgebung den Zustand des Unterwegsseins unterbrechen und kleine Reisestappen definieren, würden Obdachlose. Deren Fähigkeit, allerorten eine Art von Zuhause einzurichten, verweist auf den Verlust ihres ursprünglichen Heimes – während in den Bildern Koen Vermeulens nur eine zeitweise Abwesenheit von diesen vertrauten und geschützten Orten angenommen werden muss. In den aufgezählten Bildern wird also ein für die zeitgenössischen Gesellschaften markantes und global verbreitetes Merkmal festgehalten. Es handelt sich dabei um einen mobilen, nomadischen Lebensstil. Im Sinne dieser Argumentation ist auch die Position wichtig, die der Maler gegenüber seinen Motiven einnimmt.

Aus seiner Malperspektive lässt sich ablesen, dass die dargestellten Raumbesetzungen akzeptiert und respektiert werden. Das geschieht durch eine merkwürdige Vermischung der Perspektive und der Details, die genau betrachtet nicht logisch ist, aber dennoch, so wie sie ins Bild eingebracht wurde, vollkommen selbstverständlich erscheint. In *Island* zum Beispiel sitzen zwei Mädchen nebeneinander auf einem Steinboden. Das weiter hinten sitzende hat einen kleinen Koffer vor sich abgelegt, der nun als rosafarbener, mit schwarzen Sternen dekorierter Tisch für ihren Laptop dient. Sie schaut in Richtung des Displays, das sie leicht zur Seite gedreht hat, wie um ihrer Freundin den Blick darauf zu ermöglichen. Jenes zweite Mädchen aber ist mit einem kleinen Stoffbeutel beschäftigt, an dem sie in größter Ruhe zu nesteln scheint, mit einer Geduld, wie sie aus dem Gefühl entsteht, momentan durch

here is a mobile, nomadic lifestyle. For the purpose of this discussion, the position the artist assumes when facing his subjects is also important.

From his point of view as an artist we can gather that the occupations of space that he portrays are accepted and respected. That happens through a remarkable mixture of perspective and details, which when examined carefully is not logical, but yet appears completely natural in the way it has been incorporated into the picture. In *Island* for example, two girls are sitting side by side on a stone floor. The girl sitting further towards the back has placed a small suitcase in front of her, which now serves as a pink laptop table decorated with black stars. She is looking at the display, which she has twisted to one side, as if to permit her friend to take a look. However, the second girl is busy with a small cloth bag, with which she seems to be calmly fiddling, so that she appears to give us the impression that at the moment she has nothing more important to do in her life. Although she pays no attention to the display her friend is showing her, she nonetheless does not turn away from her. Not only is she sitting very close to her; she has also tucked her right arm under the left one of her companion. Her posture, sitting cross-legged, is a bit problematic in view of the short skirt she is wearing. However, not only does she seem to be completely unperturbed by this; above all, she seems to have taken possession of a space which is her own and which she is completely familiar with, in other words a sort of temporary home which

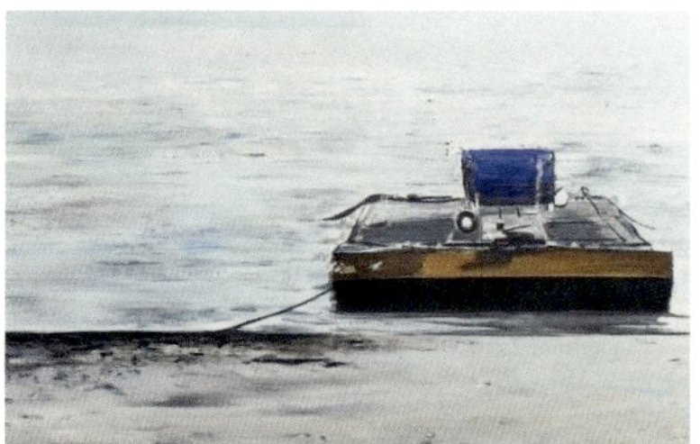

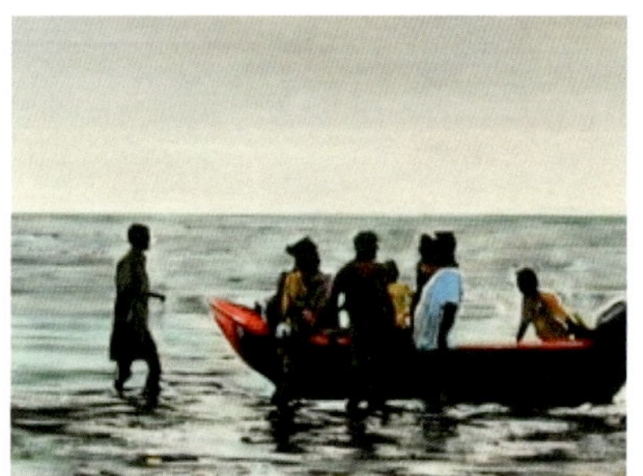

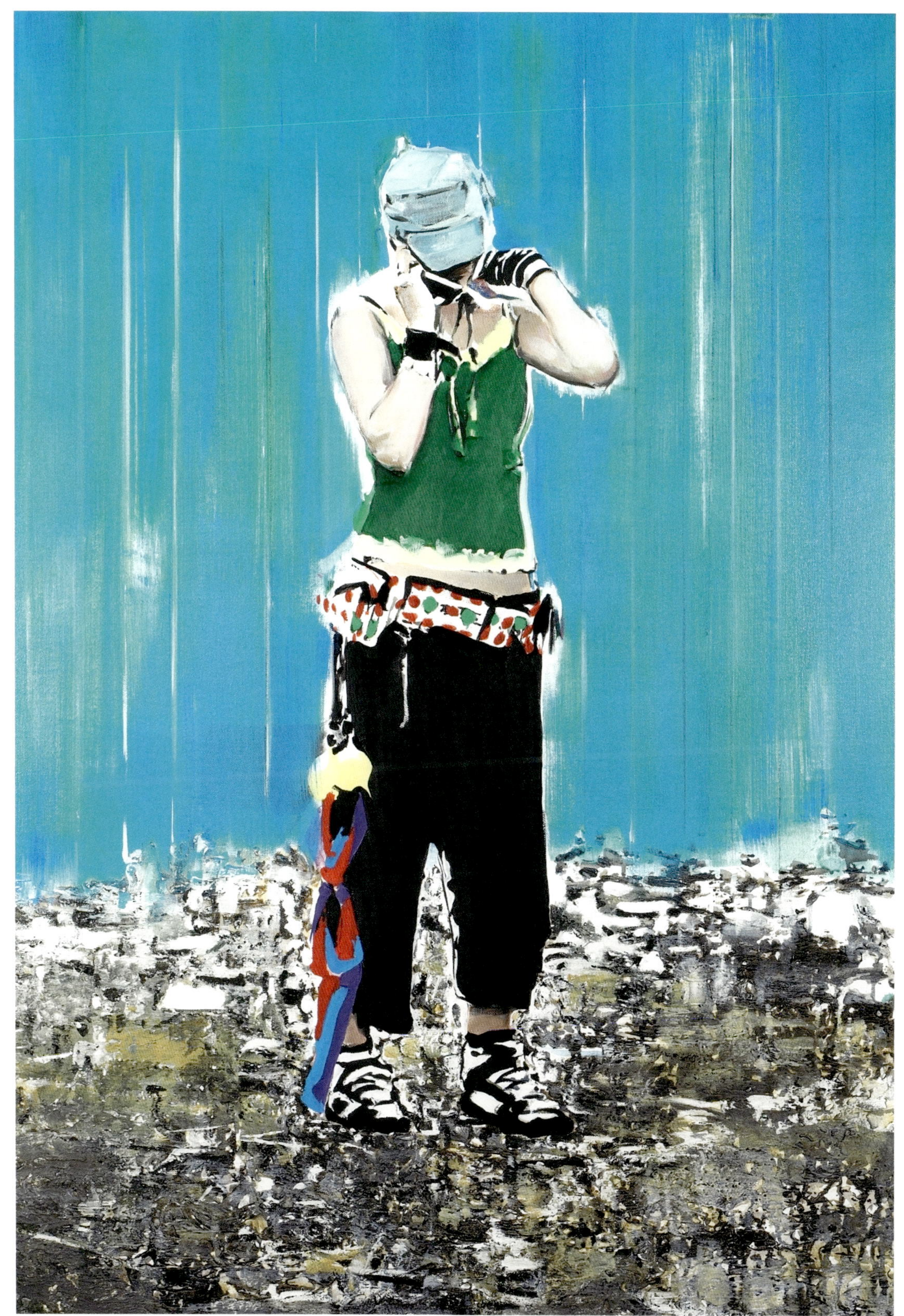

Le Depart, 2011
96,3*250,4 cm, Öl und Acryl auf Leinwand

5.oo pm, 2004
200*270 cm, Öl auf Leinwand

Global Nomad 1, 2008
145*105 cm, Öl und Acryl auf Leinwand

nichts Dringenderes zur Teilnahme am Lebensstrom verpflichtet zu sein. Während sie sich dem angebotenen Display nicht zuwendet, wendet sie sich doch von der Freundin nicht ab. Sie sitzt nicht nur sehr nah bei ihr, sondern sie hat auch ihren rechten Arm dem linken ihrer Begleiterin untergehakt. Ihre Haltung im Schneidersitz wird durch den kurzen Rock, den sie trägt, etwas heikel. Aber sie scheint deswegen nicht nur völlig unbekümmert zu sein. Sondern vor allem scheint sie einen ihr ganz vertrauten, eigenen Raum einzunehmen, eben eine Art selbstgeschaffener temporärer Heimat. Aus einem Tuch hat sie sich sogar eine Sitzfläche gestaltet, sozusagen als Rudiment eines möblierten Heimes, mit dessen Stoff sie sich gegenüber dem öffentlichen Terrain abgrenzt.

Die Vorstellung einer temporär eingerichteten Heimat ist hier mit dem Begriff der "Insel", so auch der Titel des Bildes, verknüpft. Nun ist eine Insel eine durchaus widersprüchliche Form der Heimat. Für Schiffbrüchige – betrachtet man das Wort zunächst in seinem ursprünglichen maritimen Kontext – verbindet sie mit dem glücklichen Erreichen des meerumspülten Landes den vorangegangenen Verlust von Sicherheit. Mit der Rettung winkt eine neu gewonnene, aber auch fremde Heimat, deren unverhoffte Besiedelung den Charakter einer Gefangenschaft annehmen kann. Zugleich wird mit dem Begriff der Insel auch ein traumverlorener Ort abseits gesellschaftlicher Normen bezeichnet. Hier wird das isolierte Landstück zur Plattform individueller wie auch gesellschaftlicher Utopien. Eines der Urbilder eines solchen Inseltraumes liefert Thomas Morus' *Utopia*. [3]

Um noch einmal an die Konstellation der Details zu erinnern, in der die zwei Mädchen gemalt wurden – das vertrauliche Unterhaken der Arme, der Schneidersitz in kurzem Rock, das Tuch, der Koffer, usw. – so inszeniert der Maler damit solche Inseleigenschaften wie Abgeschiedenheit, Unerreichbarkeit, Gestrandetsein, Aufenthalt außerhalb der gewöhnlichen Gesellschaft, ein von Elementen umspültes und deshalb außerhalb ihres Stroms bestehendes Dasein. Wie sind nun die Details auf sonderbare Weise mit der Darstellungsperspektive vermischt? Um die beiden Mädchen bleibt ein Raum, ein Abstand, durch den die Position der beiden respektiert wird (das gilt ebenso für *Tokyo Dreamer* und *Glasshouse)*. Die Perspektive, in welcher der Blick auf die Mädchen inszeniert wird, entspricht aber nicht dem öffentlichen Blick. Gemeint ist damit der hypothetische Blickwinkel vorübergehender Passanten. Deren Blickpunkt müsste höher liegen. Würden diejenigen, die das Bild betrachten, dieselbe Perspektive einnehmen wie der an den Mädchen vorbeiführende (und im Bild unsichtbare) Strom von Passanten, müssten die beiden in einer leichten Draufsicht gemalt sein. Das sind sie aber nicht. Stattdessen nehmen die Bildbetrachtenden eine Position den Mädchen gegenüber ein. Und zwar so, als würden sie selbst gleichfalls auf dem Boden hocken. So als würden sie nicht zu dem Strom der Passanten gehören, den sie allerdings in

she has created for herself. She has even used a cloth to mark out her space, the basic rudiments of a furnished home so to speak, using the cloth to define her territory in contrast to the public space.

The idea of a temporarily established home is linked here with the term "island" which is also the title of the picture. Now, an island is a contradictory sort of homeland. For those who have been shipwrecked – let us consider this word initially in its original maritime context – it connects the fortunate arrival on a patch of land surrounded by sea with the previous loss of safety. With this rescue there beckons a newly acquired but as yet still foreign home, whose unexpected settlement can take on the character of an imprisonment. At the same time the concept of the island also describes an idyllic place beyond the norms of society. Here the isolated patch of land becomes a platform for individual and social utopias. One of the original images of such a dream-like island can be found in Thomas More's *Utopia*. [3]

Let us recall the constellation of the details in which the two girls were painted: the intimate linking of arms, the crossed legs combined with the short skirt, the cloth, the suitcase, etc. In this manner the artist is staging island characteristics such as remoteness, inaccessibility, stranded-ness, spending time outside normal society, an existence surrounded by the elements and thus beyond the current of their existence. But how are these details mixed in a curious manner with the representational perspective? Around the two girls there remains a space, a gap by means of which their position is respected. (The same thing applies to *Tokyo Dreamer* and *Glasshouse*.) The perspective in which this view of the girls is staged does not correspond with the public view. That means the hypothetical viewing angle of temporary passers-by. Their vantage point would, in fact, be higher. If the viewers observing the picture were to adopt the same perspective as the passers-by streaming past the girls (but invisible in the picture), they would have to have been painted in a slight topview. But that is not the case. Instead, the viewers take up a position opposite the girls – a position, in fact, as if they too were sitting on the floor. As if they did not belong to the stream of passers-by whom, however, they are automatically imitating in the moment in which they stroll past the picture. This is a remarkable contradiction.

It is therefore interesting to see what happens when the picture itself is placed in a different location. If it leaves its position in a public place (the wall in a gallery or museum) and is installed in an inhabited room, beside the coffee table for example, then the people who sit down in front of the picture also take up a different position. They would reflect the position of the girls sitting in the picture through their own position in front of the picture. In

dem Moment, in welchem sie an dem Bild vorbei schlendern, automatisch imitieren. Das ist ein beachtlicher Widerspruch.

Interessant ist deshalb, was passiert, wenn das Bild selbst einer Ortsveränderung unterworfen wird. Verlässt es seinen Platz an einem öffentlichen Ort (der Wand in einer Galerie oder in einem Museum) und wird in einem bewohnten Raum installiert, sagen wir neben einem Couchtisch, dann nehmen diejenigen, die sich vor dem Bild niederlassen, selbst eine andere Position ein. Sie würden dann durch ihre eigene Position vor dem Bild die Position der sitzenden Mädchen im Bild reflektieren. In der Spiegelung dieser Positionen vor und im Bild würden die Bildbetrachtenden selbst auf eine Art Insel umziehen. Und diese Insel liegt dann zu jener der beiden Mädchen genau parallel.

Wohin die Reise in *Le Depart* (Abreise, Aufbruch) geht, ist völlig offen. Zu sehen ist nur ein Floß. Es ist nahe des schwarz-grauen Strandes mit einem Seil festgemacht. Auf dem Floß ist ein blaues Fass installiert. Es ist für Lebensmittel und trockene Kleidung vorgesehen. Wer sie brauchen wird, ist ungewiss, denn der Strand und das Wasser um das Floß herum sind leer. Das einsam schwimmende Objekt wirkt wie die Essenz einer unvollendeten Reise und vielleicht gehört es Menschen, die darauf ihr Leben riskieren werden, um die Fahrt in eine bessere Welt zu wagen.

[1] Siehe dazu zum Beispiel: Reichert, Ramón: „Das Geschlecht der Grenze. Genderrepräsentationen von der Berliner Mauer bis zur EU-Außengrenze" in: Dennerlein, Bettina und Elke Frietsch (Hrsg.), *Identitäten in Bewegung. Migration im Film, Bielefeld*, 2011, S. 35-56

[2] Bierens, Cornel: „Periferie en focus in het werk van Koen Vermeule / Periphery and focus in the work of Koen Vermeule", in: Vermeule, Koen, *High above ground*, Zwolle: WBOOKS, 2012, S. 86

[3] Siehe: Morus, Thomas, *Utopia*, Leipzig 1986. Für den Umschlag wurde der Titelholzschnitt der Erstausgabe von 1516 verwendet, der eine Insel zeigt.

the mirroring of these positions in front of and in the picture, the viewers would move onto a sort of island themselves. And this island would then lie exactly parallel to the island of the two girls.

It is completely open where the journey in *Le Départ* (departure) is heading. All we can see is a raft. It is moored with a rope just off the blackish-gray beach. A blue barrel has been installed on the raft. It is intended for food and dry clothing. It is uncertain who will need them, because the beach and the water surrounding the raft are both empty. This lonely floating object looks like the essence of an unfinished journey, and perhaps it belongs to people who will risk their lives on it and venture to make the voyage into a better world.

[1] See here, for example: Ramón Reichert: "Das Geschlecht der Grenze. Genderrepräsentationen von der Berliner Mauer bis zur EU-Außengrenze," in: Bettina Dennerlein / Elke Frietsch (eds.), Identitäten in Bewegung. Migration im Film, Bielefeld: transcript, 2011, pp. 35-56

[2] Cornel Bierens: "Periferie en focus in het werk van Koen Vermeule / Periphery and focus in the work of Koen Vermeule," in: Koen Vermeule, High above ground, Zwolle: WBOOKS, 2012, p. 86

[3] See: Thomas More, Utopia, Leipzig: Verlag Philip Reclam jun., 1986. For the cover the woodcut of the title of the first edition of 1516 was used; it shows an island.

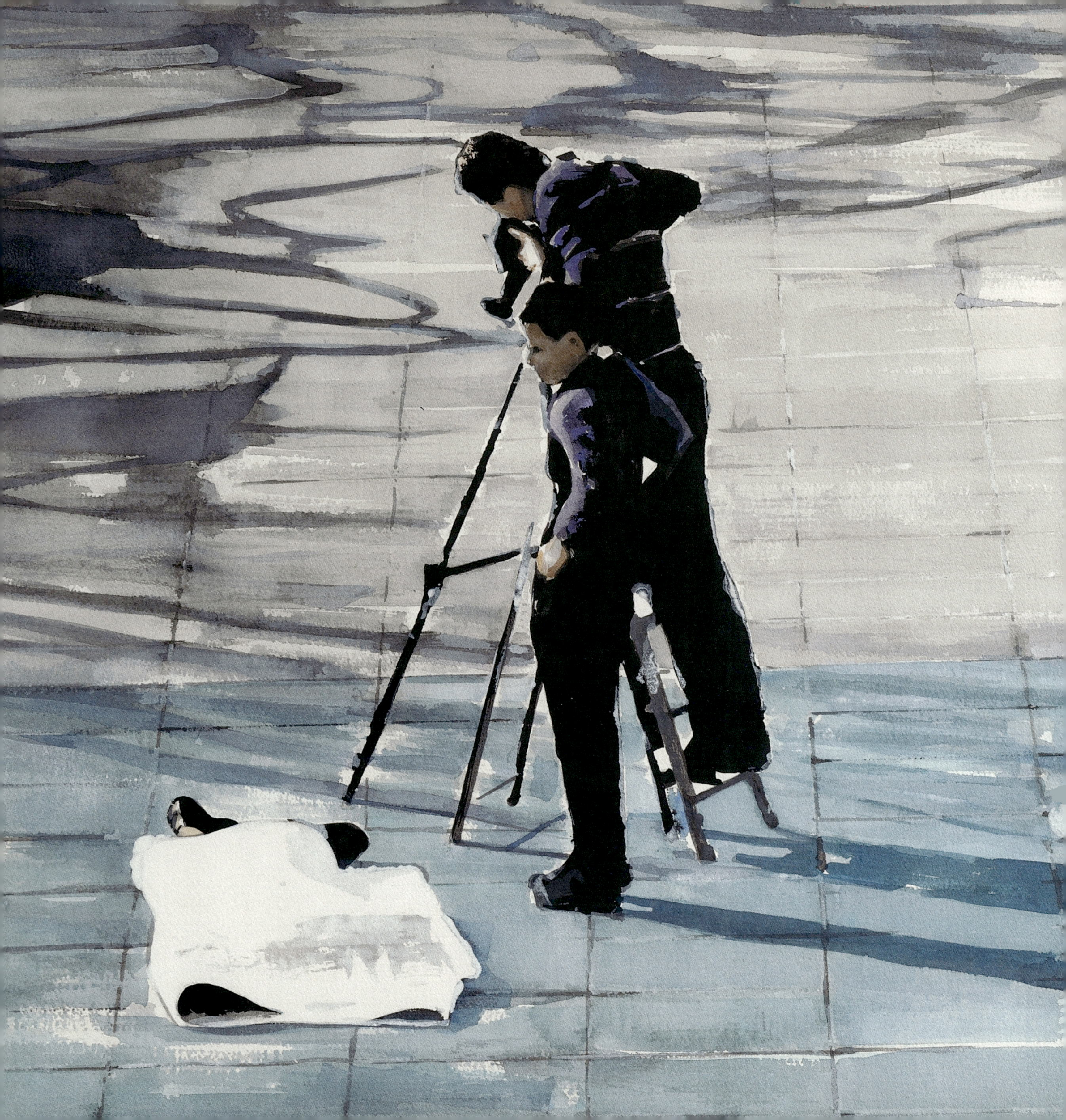

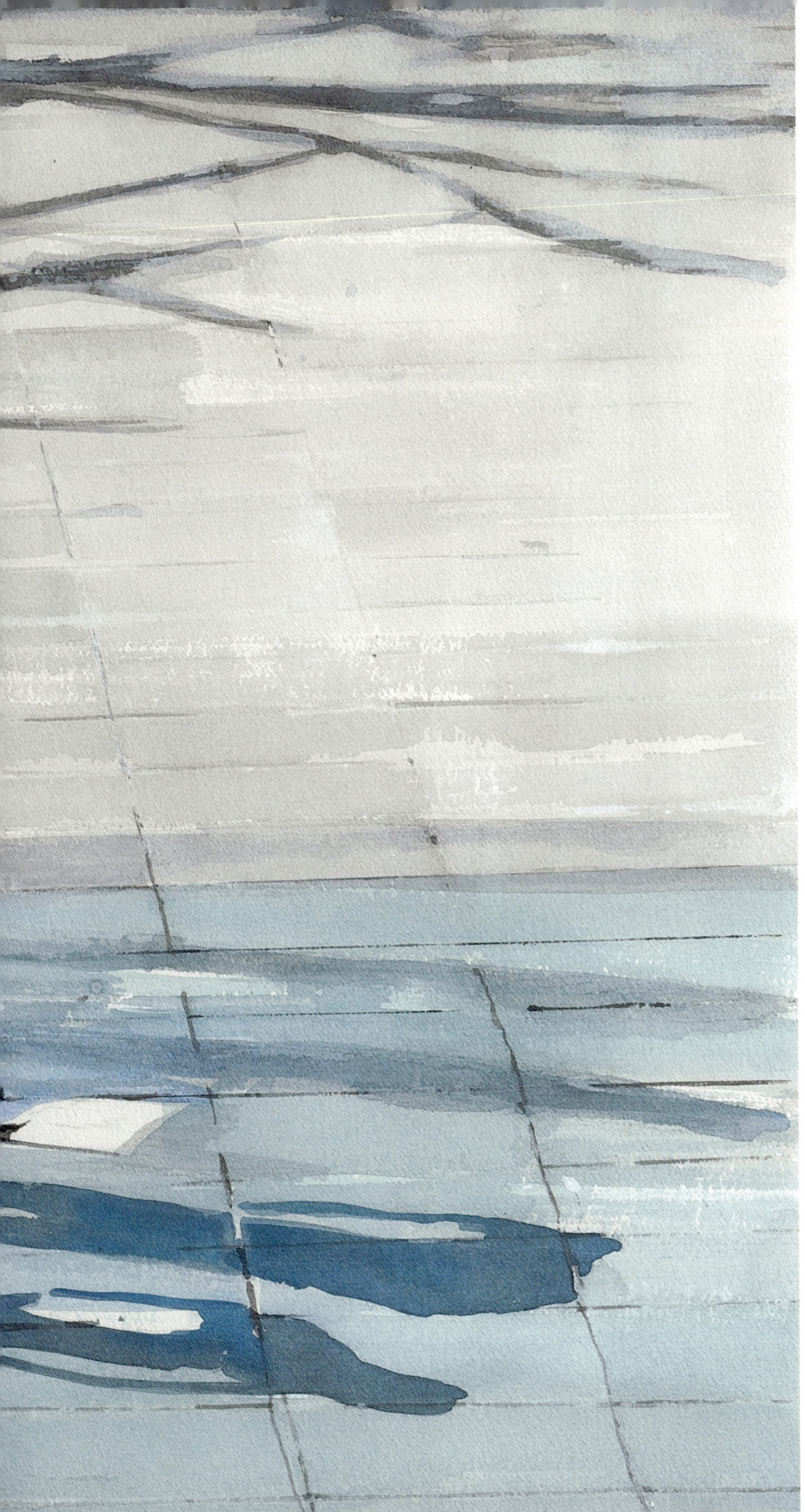

De Geuzen, 2008
65*101 cm, Gouache auf Papier

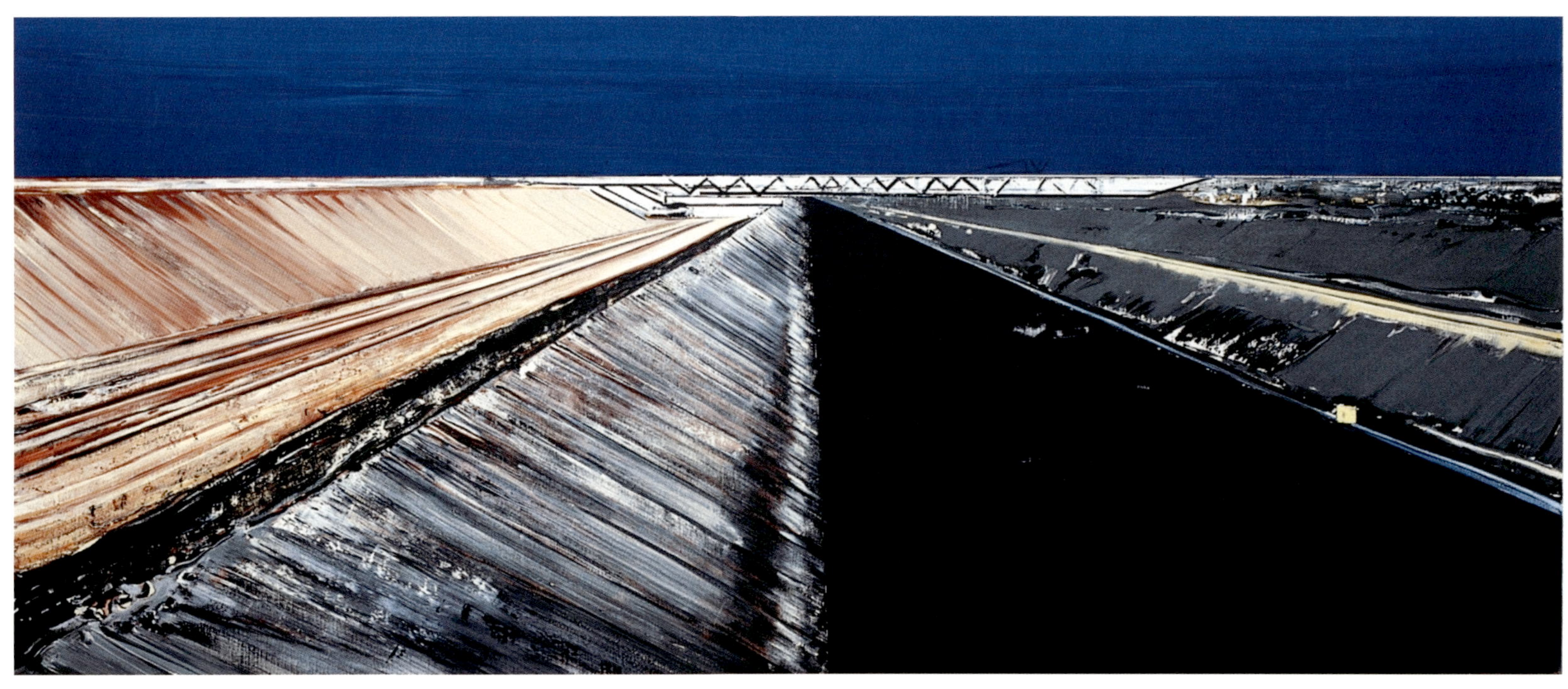

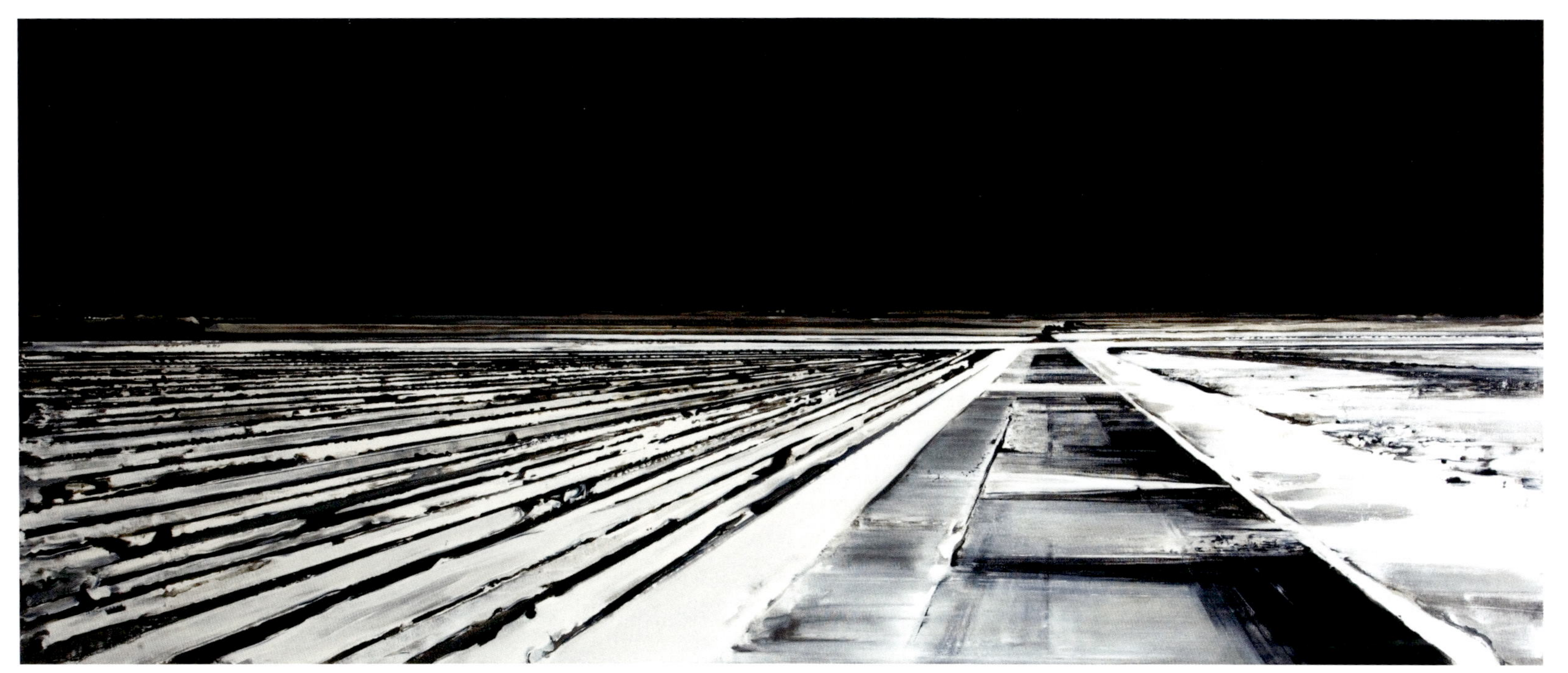

Nachtlandschaft, 2000
125*270 cm, Öl und Acryl auf Leinwand

Endless, 2010
125*300 cm, Öl und Acryl auf Leinwand

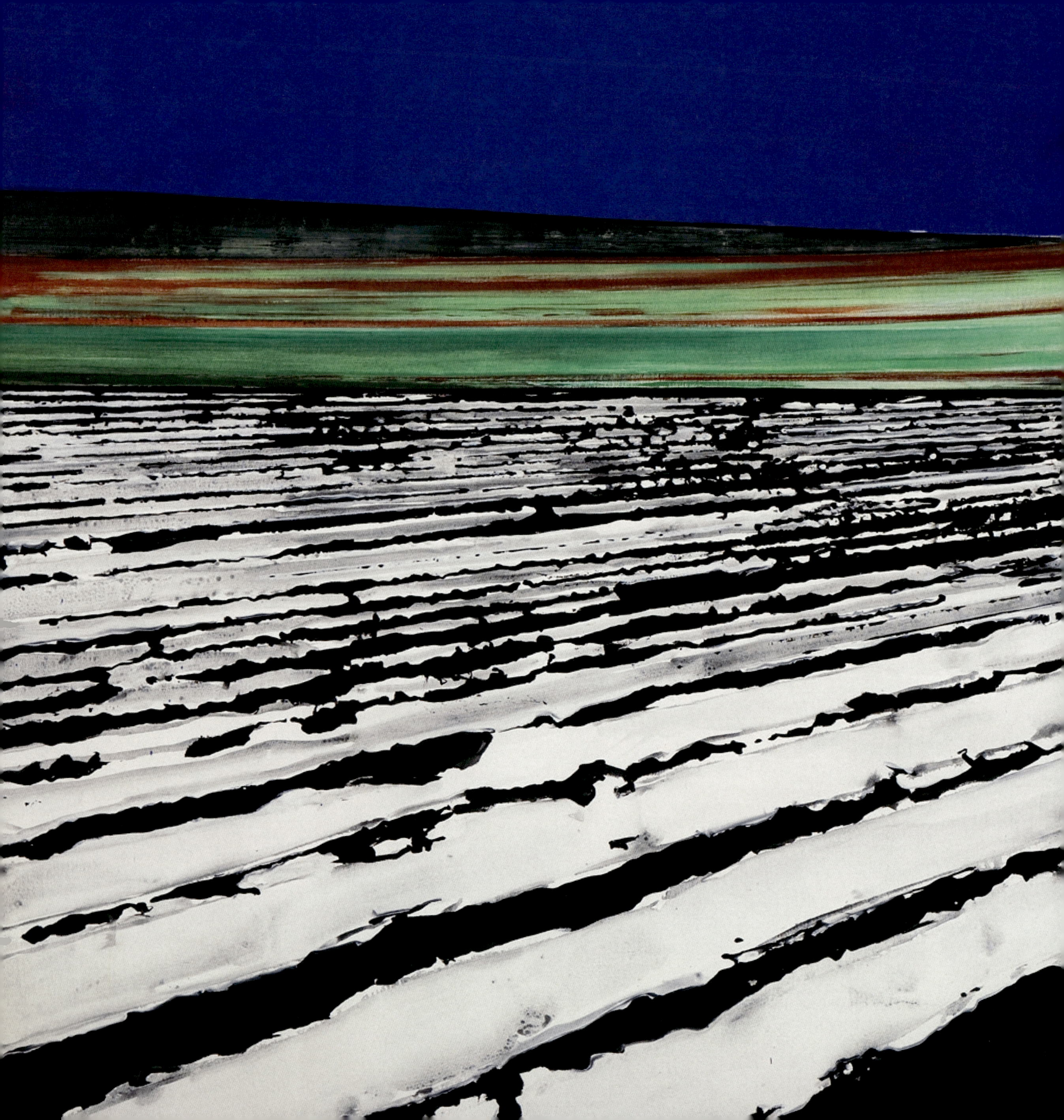

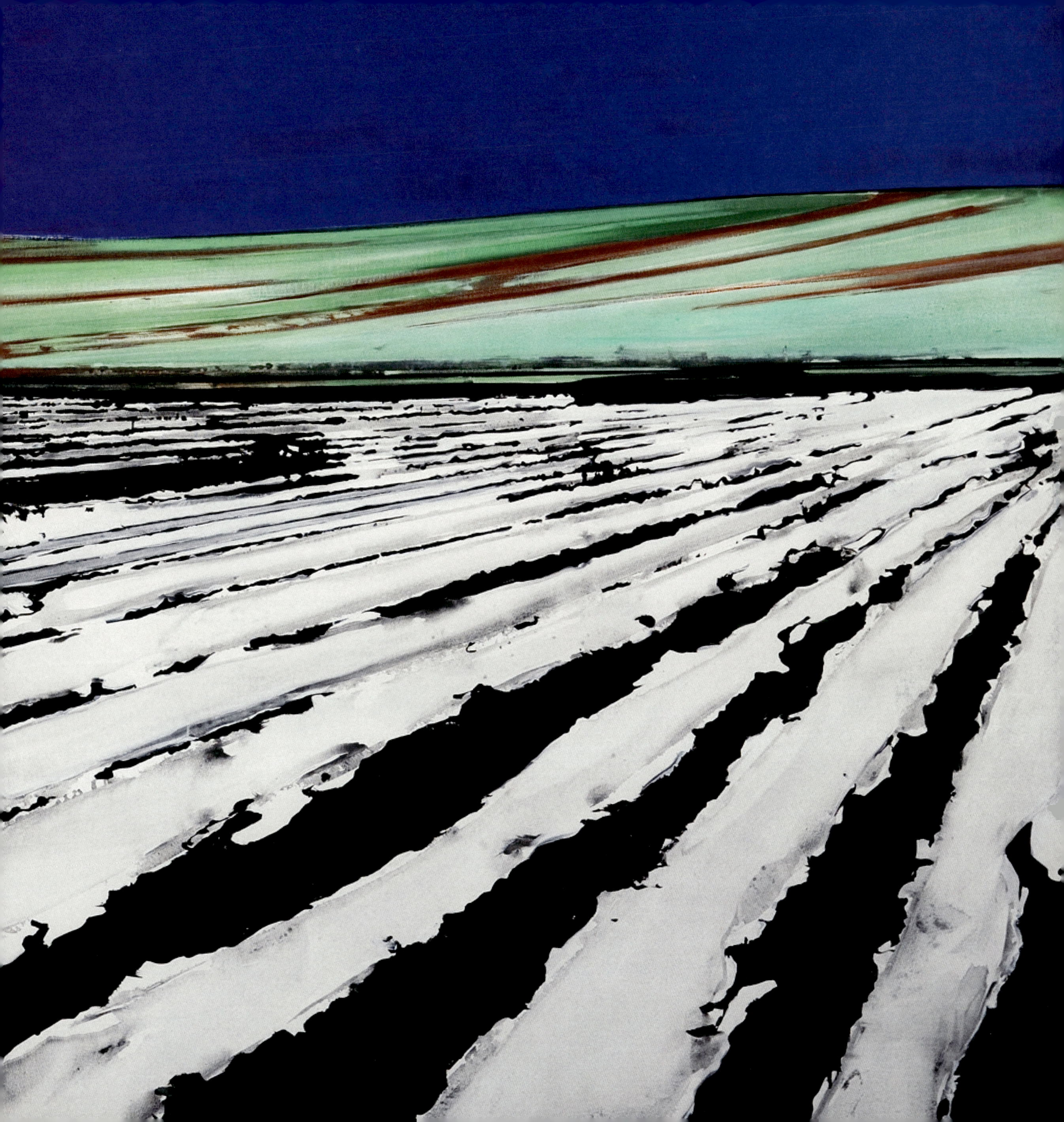

Scape, 2011
200*360 cm, Öl und Acryl auf Leinwand

Departure, 2005
210*200 cm, Öl und Acryl auf Leinwand

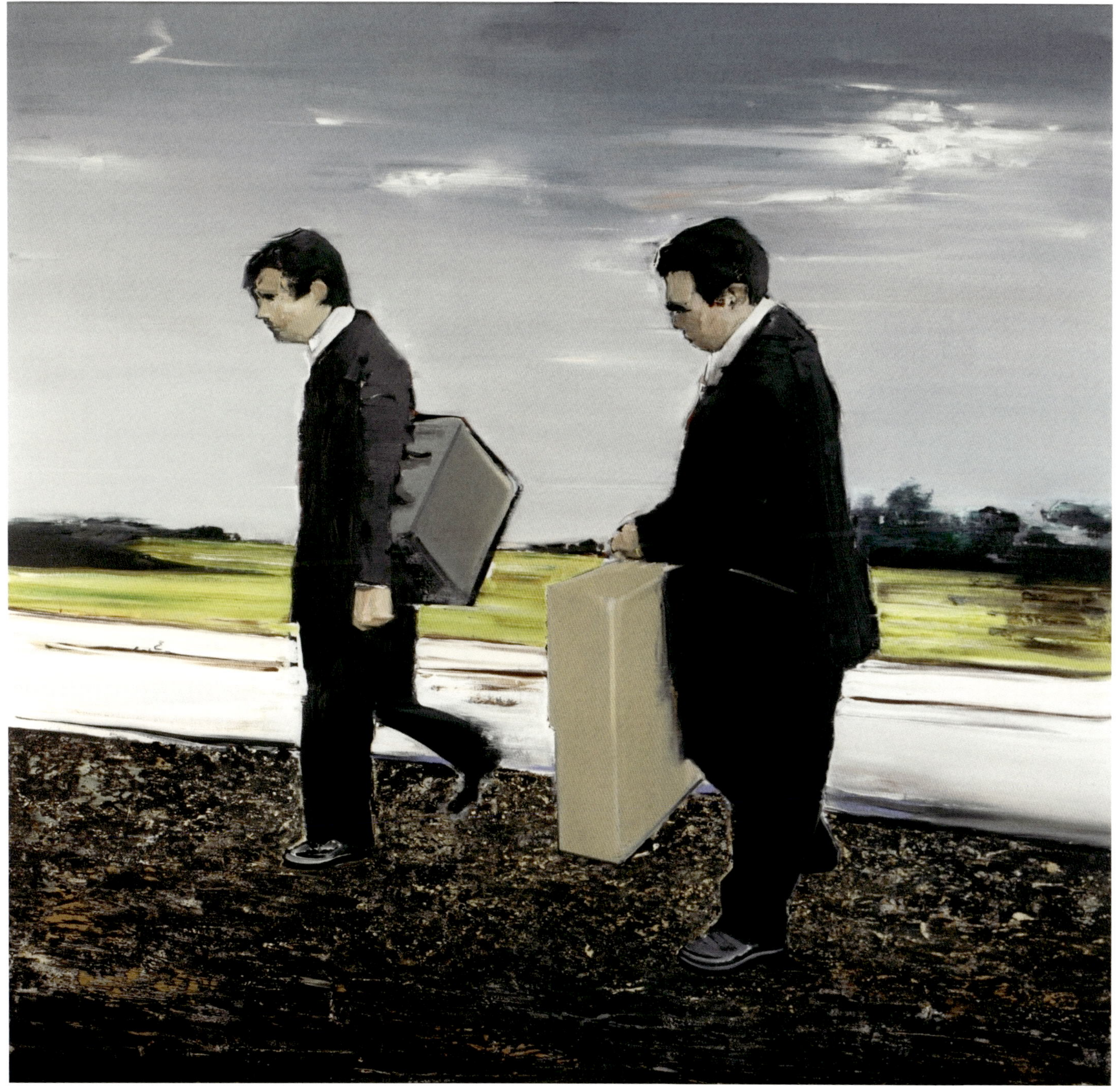

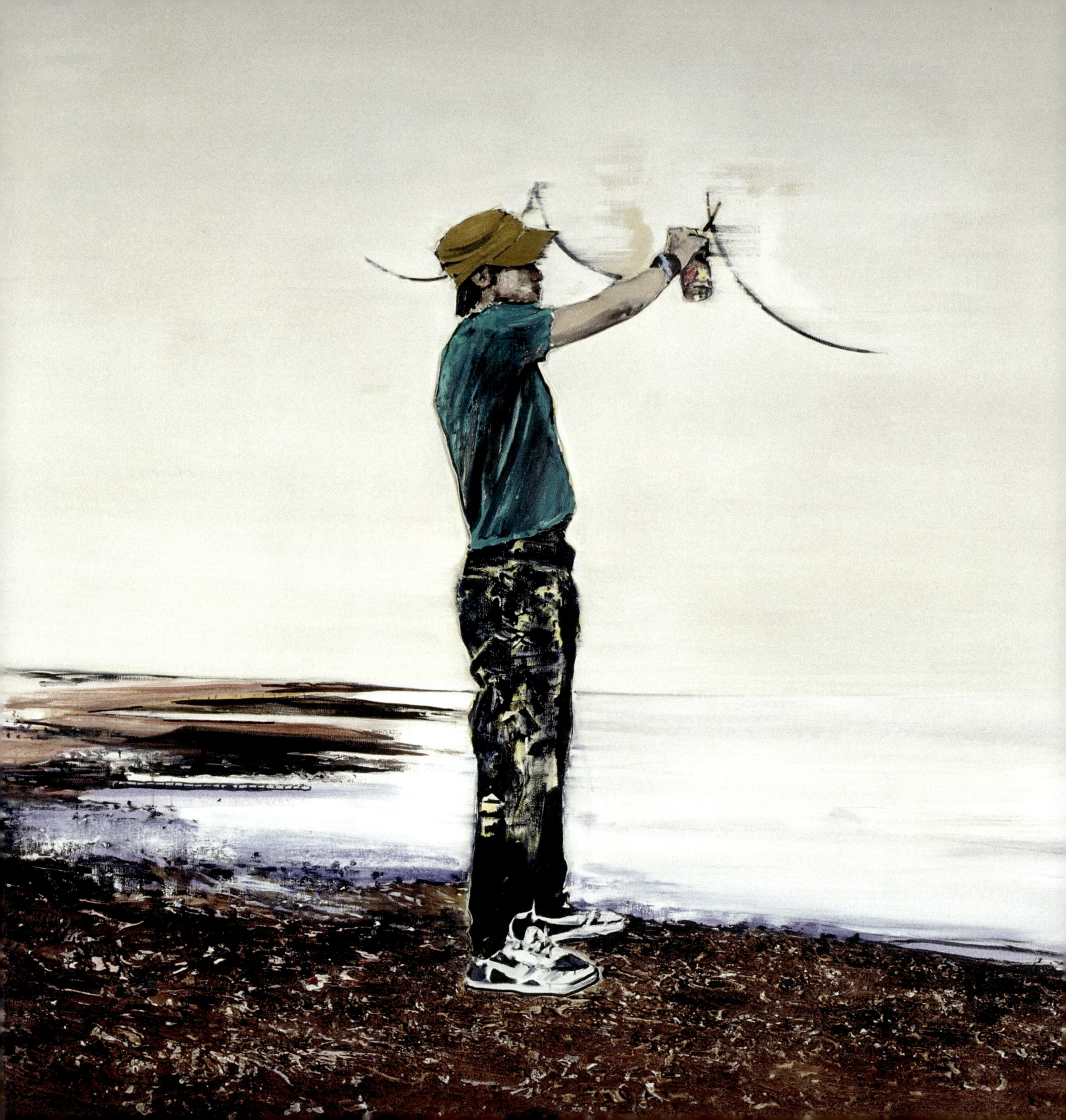

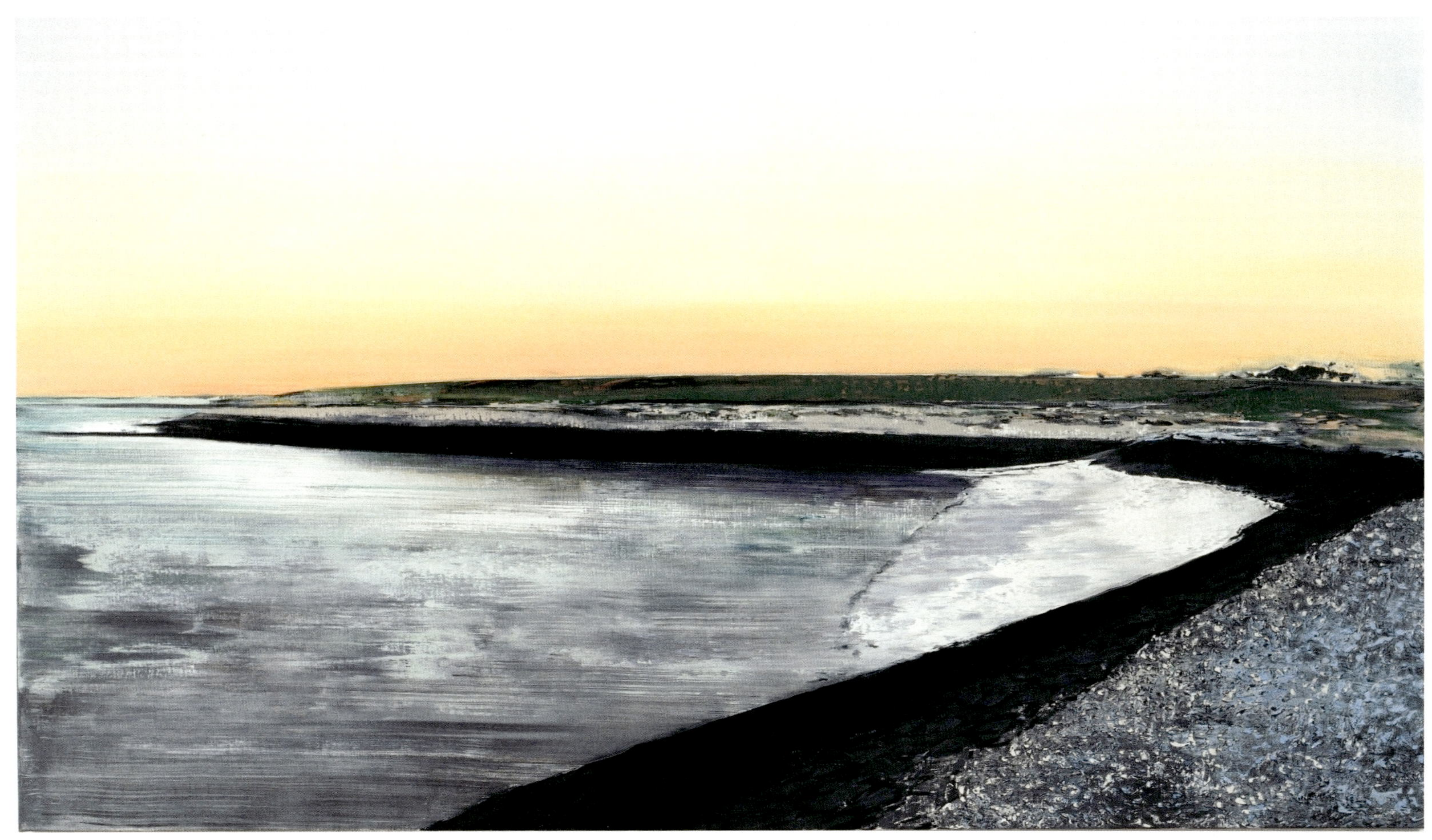

Skywriter, 2005
190*180 cm, Öl und Acryl auf Leinwand

Bay, 2002
150*270 cm, Öl und Acryl auf Leinwand

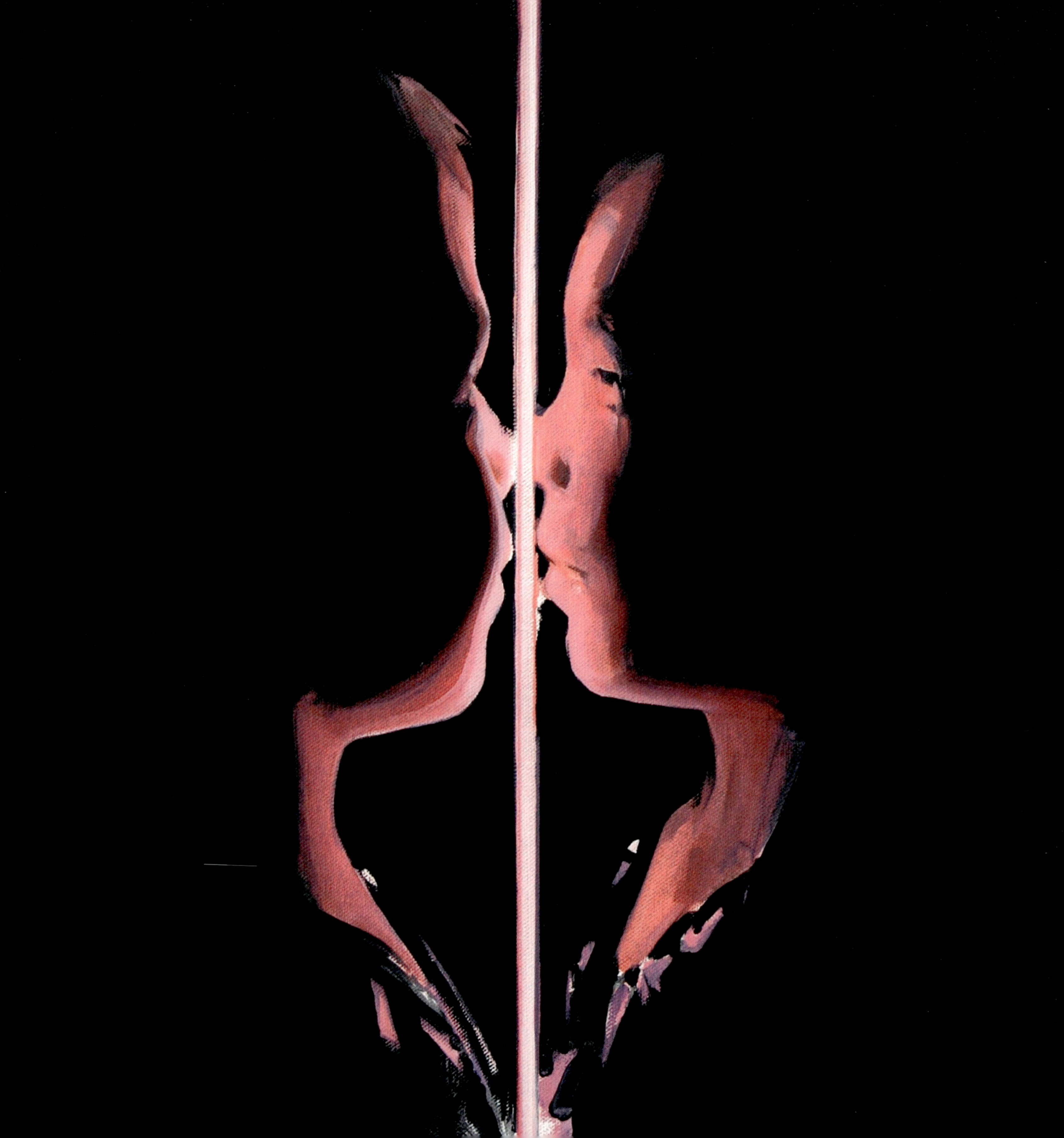

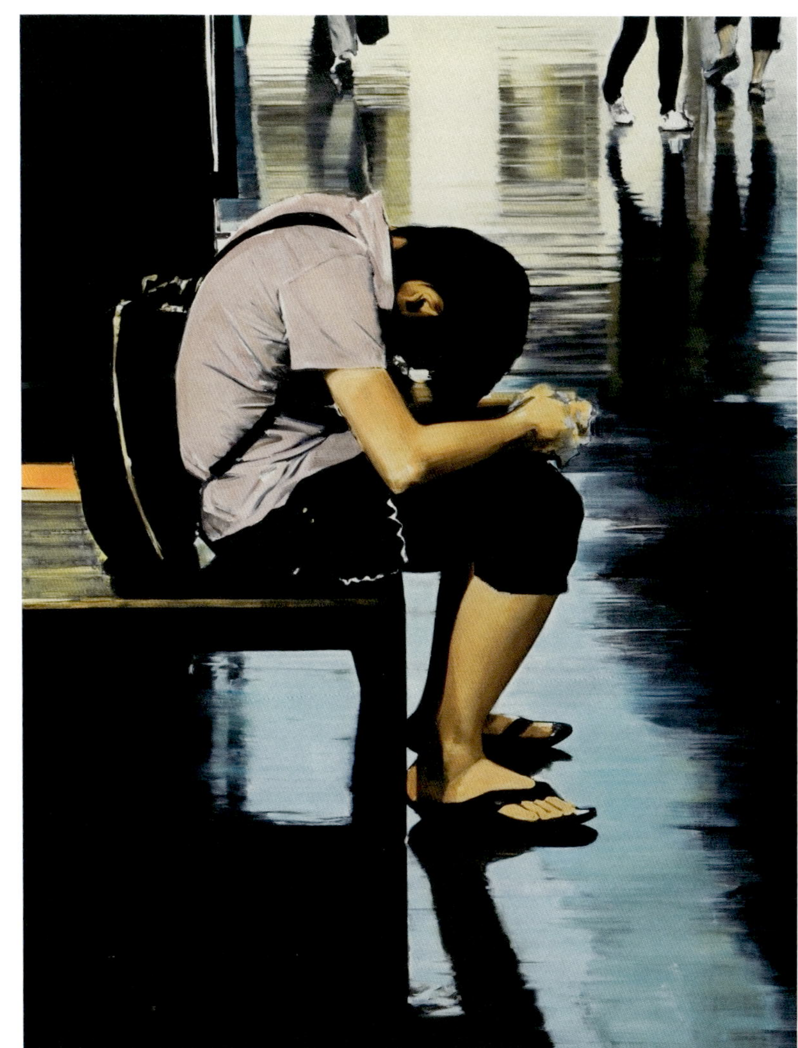

In Mirror, 2010
76*60 cm, Öl und Acryl auf Leinwand

Tokyo Dreamer, 2010
230*180 cm, Öl und Acryl auf Leinwand

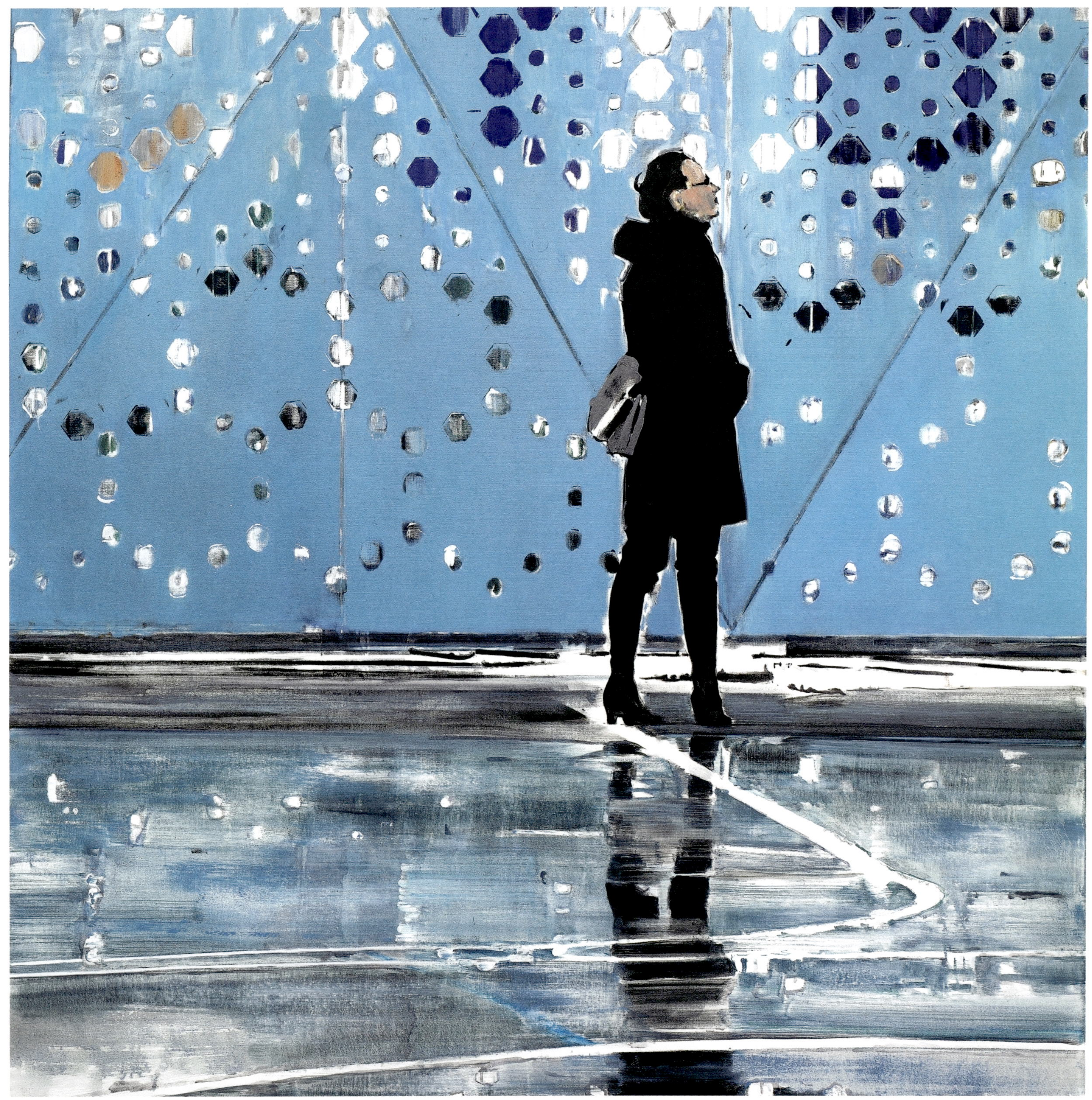

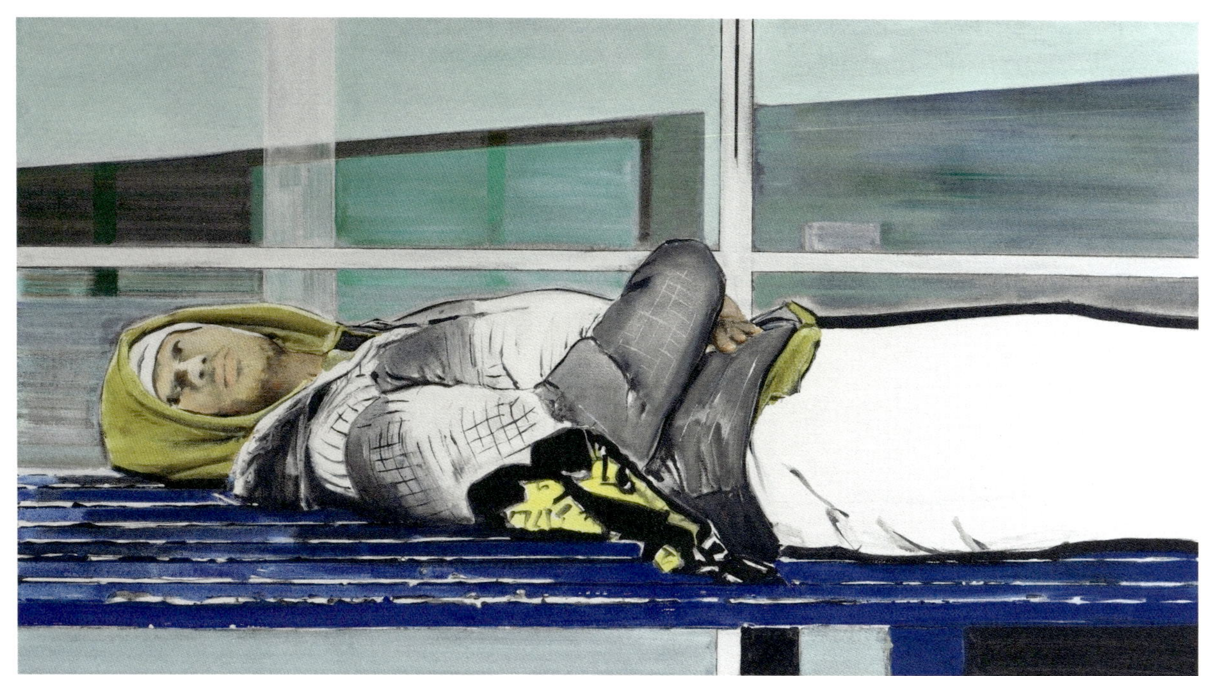

Dome, 2008
210*200 cm, Öl und Acryl auf Leinwand

Skater, 2011
75*135 cm, Öl und Acryl auf Leinwand

Hangout, 2007
55*71 cm, Gouache auf Papier

Top of the World, 2011
110*180 cm, Öl und Acryl auf Leinwand

Le Depart, 2011
96,3*250,4 cm, Öl und Acryl auf Leinwand

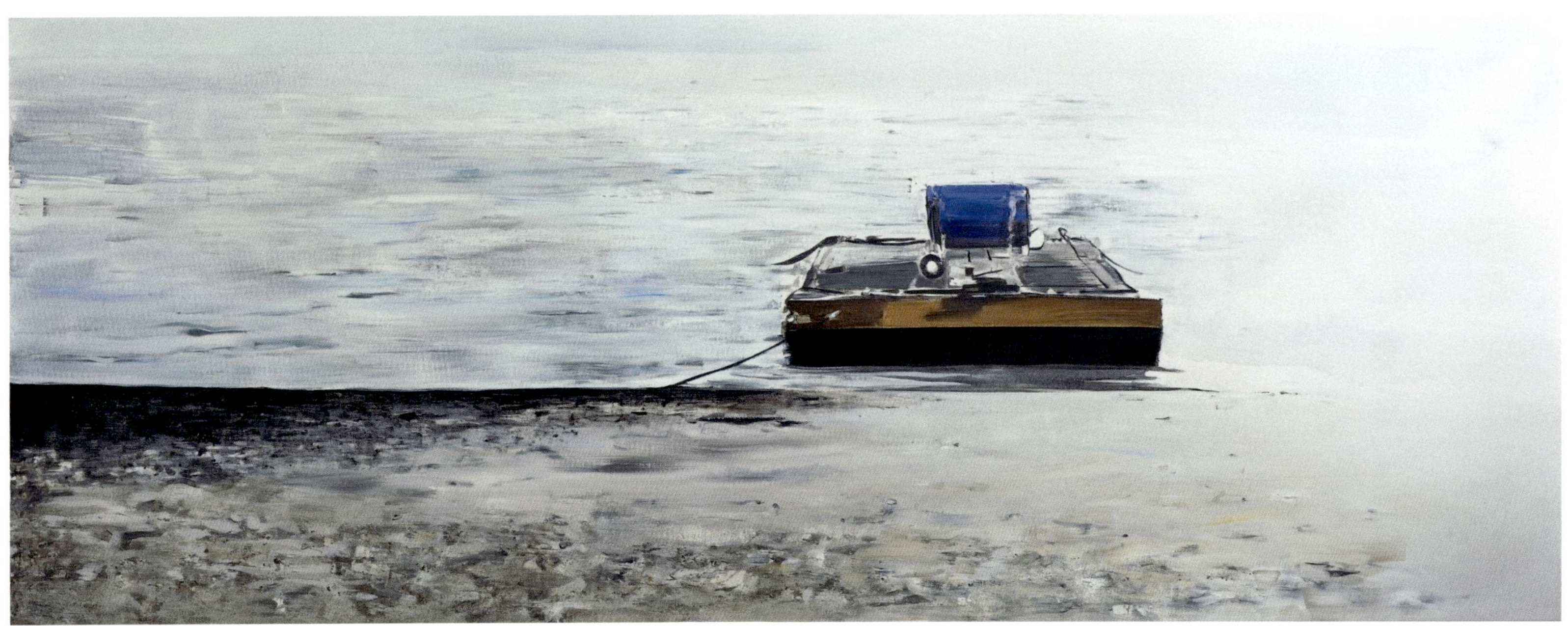

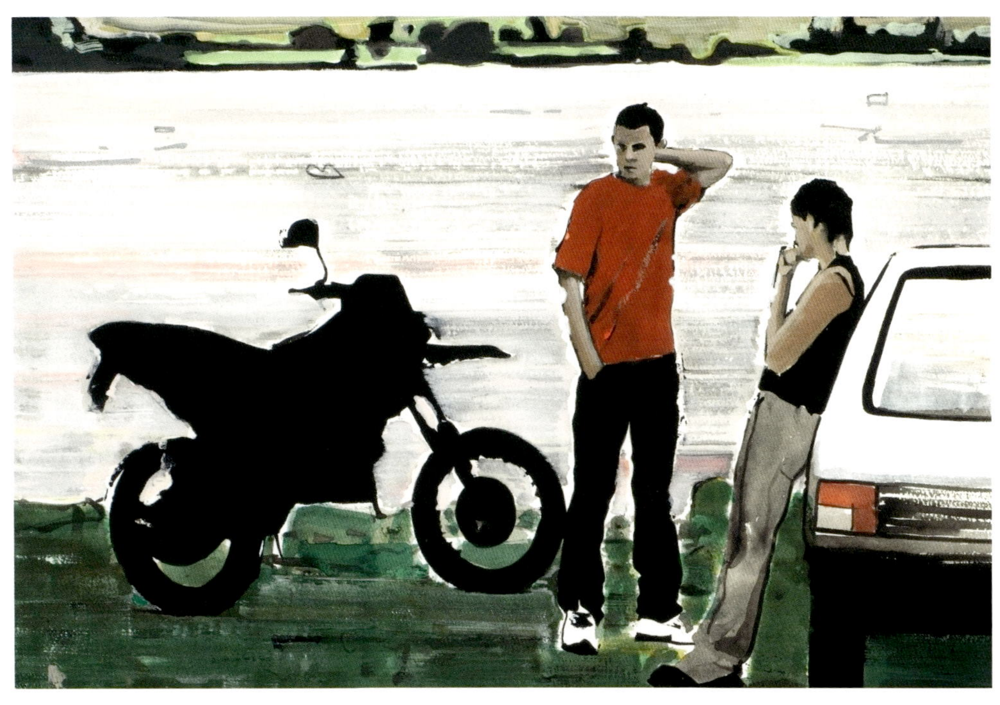

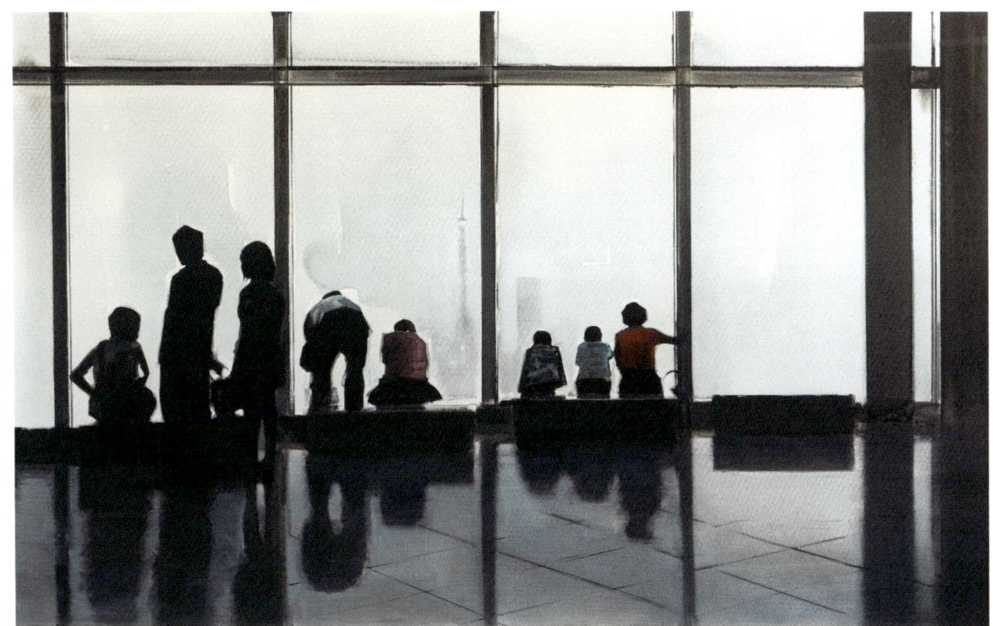

Collectors Edition

Zu diesem Buch erscheint eine Sonderedition:
Öl und Acryl auf Leinwand im Format 35*90 cm.
7 individuelle Exemplare, nummeriert und signiert.

This publication is accompanied by a special edition:
Oil and acryl on canvas, 35*90 cm.
7 individual copies, numbered and signed.

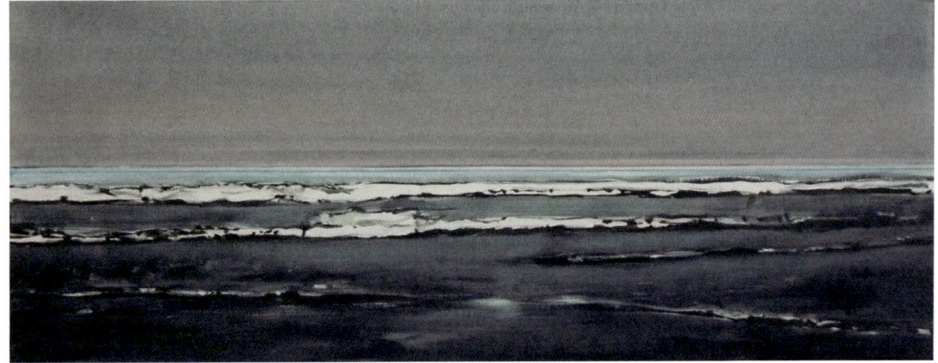

***Seascape pink*, 2012**
35*90 cm, Öl und Acryl auf Leinwand

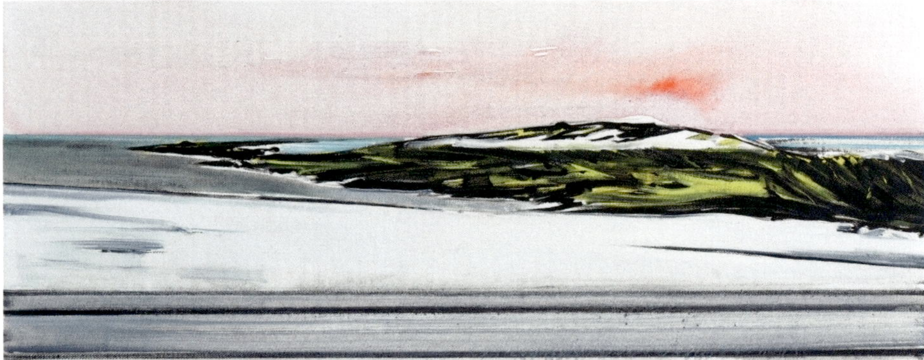

***Dune 1*, 2012**
35*90 cm, Öl und Acryl auf Leinwand

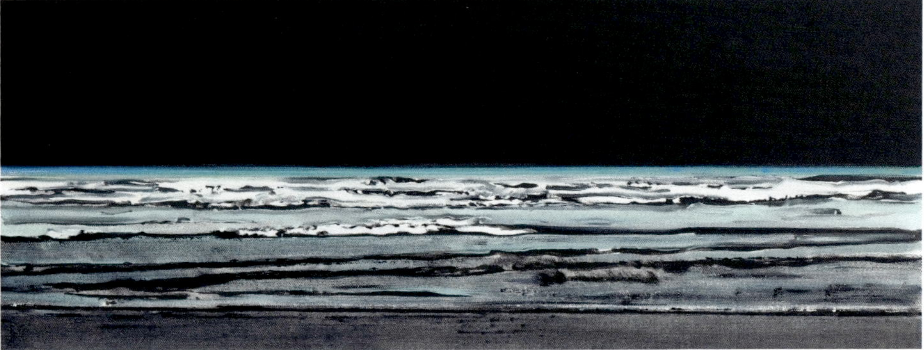

***Seascape night*, 2012**
35*90 cm, Öl und Acryl auf Leinwand

Seascape green, 2012
35*90 cm, Öl und Acryl auf Leinwand

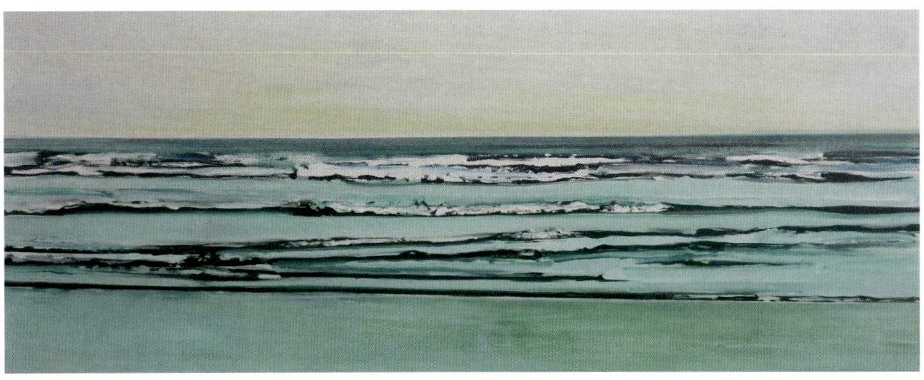

Nocturne Road, 2012
35*90 cm, Öl und Acryl auf Leinwand

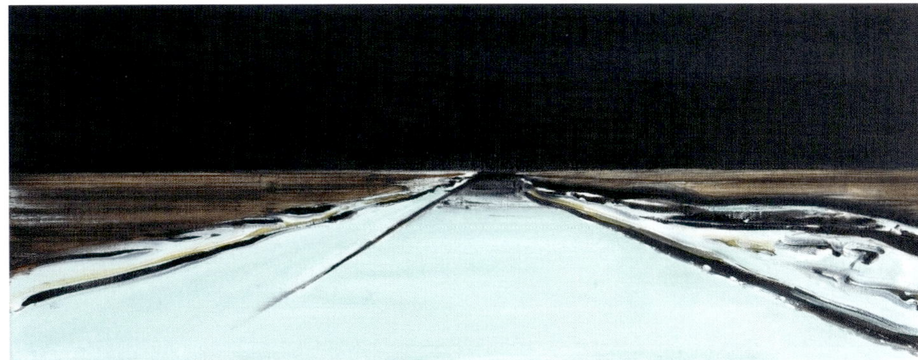

Valderobres, 2012
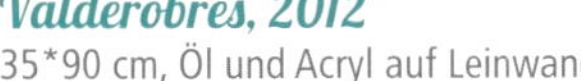
35*90 cm, Öl und Acryl auf Leinwand

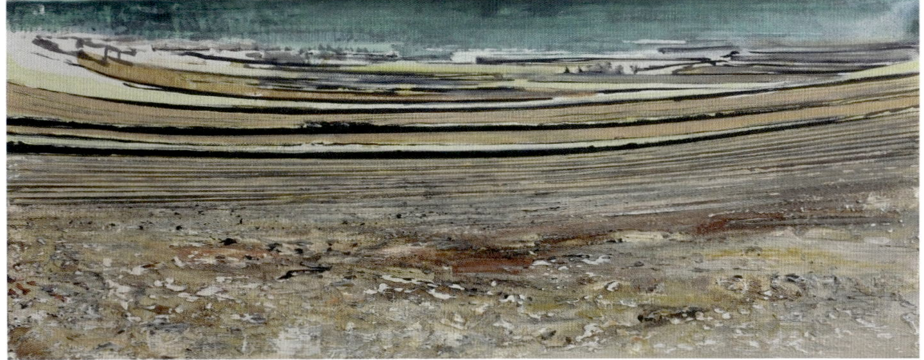

Dune 2, 2012
35*90 cm, Öl und Acryl auf Leinwand

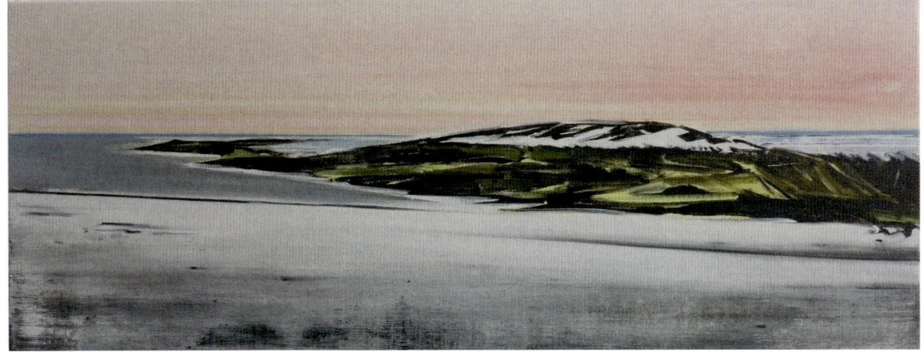

Inhalt/Content

Bilder in Museen, Galerien und Sammlungen/Works in museums, galleries and collections:
CALDIC Collection, Wassenaar S. 36/37; Centraal Museum, Utrecht S. 67; Gemeentemuseum Helmond: S. 32; ING Collection Nederland S. 70; Kunstmuseum Dieselkraftwerk, Cottbus S. 60; Privatsammlungen; S. 14/15, S. 16/17, S. 22, S. 24/25, S. 28, S. 32 S. 43, S. 55, S. 61, S. 65, S. 66, S. 68, S. 73; Rijksmuseum Twenthe, on loan No Hero Foundation, Enschede S.46; SCHUNCK*, Glaspaleis, Heerlen S. 47; Staatliche Kunstsammlungen Dresden, Galerie Neue Meister (donated by Karen Hänel and Bernd Bilitewski): S. 23; Staatliche Kunstsammlungen Dresden, Galerie Neue Meister, on loan from the Gesellschaft für Moderne Kunst in Dresden e. V.: S. 44/45, 69; TNT Post Kunstcollectie S. 77; Galerie Wittenbrink, München: S. 19, S. 31, S. 38/39, S. 18/19, S. 62/63, S. 71, S. 72, S. 73, S. 74/75.

Cover-Abbildung/front cover: Tokyo Dreamer, 2010 (detail)

Herausgegeben von/edited by: Jürgen Krieger
Lektorat/copy editing: Eckhard Hollmann

Übersetzung aus dem Deutschen/translation from the German: Jane Michael

Gestaltungskonzept/design concept and layout: WE ARE INDEED, www.weareindeed.com, München
Herstellung/production: Susanne Rösler, Berlin
Litho/origination: Reproline mediateam, München
Druck und Bindung/printing and binding: DZA Druckerei zu Altenburg GmbH

Die Deutsche Nationalbibliothek verzeichnet diese Publikation in der Deutschen Nationalbibliografie; detaillierte bibliografische Daten sind über das Internet abrufbar: http://dnb.d-nb.de
Die Deutsche Nationalbibliothek lists this publication in the German national bibliography, detailed bibliographic data are available on the Internet http://dnb.d-nb.de

jovis Verlag GmbH
Kurfürstenstr. 15/16
10785 Berlin
www.jovis.de

jovis books are available worldwide. Please contact your nearest bookseller or the address above for information concerning your local distribution.

Printed in Germany
ISBN: 978-3-86859-180-4